The Crimes Women Commit,
The Punishments They Receive

The Crimes
Women Commit,
The Punishments
They Receive

Rita J. Simon

AND

Jean Landis

American University

Lexington Books

D.C. Heath and Company/Lexington, Massachusetts/Toronto

Library of Congress Cataloging-in-Publication Data

Simon, Rita James.
The crimes women commit, the punishments they receive / by Rita J.
Simon and Jean Landis.
p.   cm.
Includes index.
ISBN 0-669-20236-3 (alk. paper)
1. Female offenders—United States.   2. Sex discrimination in
criminal justice administration—United States.   3. Women prisoners—
United States.   I. Landis, Jean.   II. Title.
HV6046.S54 1990

364.3′74′0973—dc20   90-6432
                                                                  CIP

Published simultaneously in Canada
Printed in the United States of America
International Standard Book Number: 0-669-20236-3
Library of Congress Catalog Card Number: 90-6432

The paper used in this publication meets
the minimum requirements of American National
Standard for Information Sciences—Permanence of Paper
for Printed Library Materials, ANSI Z39.48-1984.

Year and number of this printing:

91 92 93 94 95 8 7 6 5 4 3 2 1

Contents

Tables

Acknowledgments

The authors express their appreciation to Joyce Turner for the wonderfully efficient work she did in typing and organizing draft after draft of this manuscript. Others who assisted us in collecting data and analyzing them are Angela Musolino, Dolores Homa, and Beth Pausic.

Introduction

The first edition of *Women and Crime* was published in 1975. When it appeared, it joined only a handful of other studies that focused primarily on women's involvement in criminal activities and on how women were treated by the criminal justice system. Writing more than ten years earlier, Barbara Wooton commented:

> It is perhaps rather curious that no serious attempt has yet been made to explain the remarkable facts of the sex ratio in detected criminality; for the scale of the sex differential far outranks all the other tracts (except that of age in the case of indictable offenses) which have been supposed to distinguish the delinquent from the nondelinquent population. It seems to be one of those facts which escape notice by virtue of its very conspicuousness. It is surely, to say the least, very odd that half the population should be apparently immune to the criminogenic factors which lead to the downfall of so significant a population of the other half. Equally odd is it, too, that although the criminological experience of different countries varies considerably, nevertheless the sex differential remains (pp. 6–8).

All that has changed. Since *Women and Crime* was released in 1975, a rich and complex literature has been devoted to the issues of gender and crime, with a special focus on women's socioeconomic status and their propensity to commit various types of crimes. Studies and monographs also have been published about women in prison, with a special emphasis on their relationships with their children and their opportunities to avail themselves of vocational training and gainful employment during their stay in prison.

The references at the end of this book provide a reasonably thorough sample of the relevant work that has been published since 1975, and throughout this revised edition, we refer to studies that have been published since 1975. But since this is a second edition, its major purpose is to update the statistical data on arrests, convictions, and commitment to prisons provided in the first edition; to make the necessary changes in the data describing demographic characteristics and socioeconomic status; and to update the information about the conditions in women's prisons. We are, however, aware of the theoretical perspectives that have been developed since 1975, primarily those of a feminist, Marxist, or Marxist-feminist nature. Where appropriate, we acknowledge the differences between those theories and ours and try to present the positions of proponents of those theories.

We take a careful look at the statistics describing women's arrests for different types of offenses, women's rates of conviction by types of offense in selective states and all federal courts, and women's commitment to state and federal prisons. We analyze both the trends in the criminal justice system over a twenty-five-year period and the changes in the types of criminal activities in which women were involved.

To determine what changes have occurred, we examine indexes of women's status in American society—their educational attainment, marital status, labor force participation, and income, especially the income ratios vis-à-vis men. These demographic and socioeconomic indexes, in conjunction with arrest data, are the major sources we used to assess the validity of the explanation for changes in female crime patterns offered in the first edition (Simon 1975):

> As women become more liberated from hearth and home and become more involved in full-time jobs, they are more likely to engage in the types of crimes for which their occupations provide them with the greatest opportunities. They are also likely to become partners and entrepreneurs in crime to a greater extent than they have in the past. Traditionally, women in criminal activity have played subservient roles. They have worked under the direction and guidance of men who were their lovers, husbands, or pimps. In most instances, their job was to entice victims, to distract or look out for the police, to carry the loot, or to provide the necessary cover. As a function both of expanded consciousness, as well as occupational opportunities, women's participation, roles, and involvement in crime are expected to change and increase.
>
> But the increase will not be uniform or stable across crimes. Women's participation in financial and white collar offenses (fraud, embezzlement, larceny, and forgery) should increase as their opportunities for employment in higher status occupations expand. Women's participation in crimes of violence, especially homicide and manslaughter, are not expected to increase. The reasoning here is that women's involvement in such acts typically arises out of the frustration, the subservience, and the dependency that have characterized the traditional female role. Case histories of women who kill reveal that one pattern dominates all others. When women can no longer contain their frustrations and their anger, they express themselves by doing away with

the cause of their condition, most often a man, sometimes a child. As women's employment and educational opportunities expand, their feelings of being victimized and exploited will decrease, and their motivation to kill will become muted. (pp. 1–2)

In the two decades from 1953 to 1973, there was an increase in women's criminal activities. The increase in serious (Type I) offenses was due almost entirely to women's greater participation in property offenses, especially larceny. As for the Type II offenses, the greatest increases occurred in embezzlement and fraud and in forgery and counterfeiting. The increases were especially marked for the period from 1967 to 1972. In commenting on those data, Simon (1975) wrote: "Should the average rate of change that occurred between 1967 and 1972 continue, female arrest rates for larceny/theft, embezzlement, and fraud will be commensurate to women's representation in the society, or in other words, roughly equal to male arrest rates (p. 46). About female arrests for violent crimes, she noted, "The proportion of female arrests for violent crimes has changed hardly at all over the past two decades. Female arrest rates for homicide, for example, [have] been the most stable of all violent offenses" (p. 46).

This edition reports arrest statistics up through 1987 and provides the opportunity to examine whether the predicted increases in white-collar property offenses have in fact occurred and whether women's involvement in violent offenses have remained constant or declined.

We will try to determine whether women's participation in the labor force continued to increase and whether the type of jobs they hold shifted from those involving less responsibility, authority, and prestige to those involving more of these qualities. We argue that women in higher-status positions are more likely to have access to other people's money and are therefore in a position to commit embezzlement, fraud, and other white-collar offenses. Women's propensity to commit property offenses is in large measure a function of their greater participation in the labor force and of their mobility from lower- to higher-status white-collar positions.

Concerning women's appearance in court, Simon (1975) wrote:

Two schools of thought prevail on how women defendants are treated at the bar of justice. Most observers feel that women receive preferential treatment, which in operational terms means that they are less likely to be convicted than men for the same type of offense; if convicted, they are less likely to be sentenced; and if sentenced, they are likely to receive milder sentences. The factors that are thought to motivate judges toward leniency vis-à-vis women are chivalry, naiveté (for example, judges often say that they cannot help but compare women defendants with other women they know well; namely their mothers and wives whom they cannot imagine behaving in the manner attributed to the defendant), and practicality. Most of the women defendants have young children, and sending them to prison places too much of a burden on the rest of the society. (p. 49)

The other view about how women fare at the bar of justice is that judges are more punitive toward women. They are more likely to throw the book at the female defendant because they believe that there is a greater discrepancy between her behavior and the behavior expected of women than there is between the behavior of the male defendant and the behavior expected of men. In other words, women defendants pay for the judges' belief that it is more in man's nature to commit crimes than it is in woman's. Thus, when a judge is convinced that the woman before him has committed a crime, he is more likely to overact and punish her, not only for the specific offense, but also for transgressing against his expectations of womanly behavior. (p. 52)

Simon relied on two sources of data for evaluating these views: (1) the percentage of women versus the percentage of men found guilty for the same types of offenses, and (2) the punishment women received compared to that given men. For these data, she had to rely mainly on the federal courts and on state courts in California, New York, and Ohio. The other source of data was interviews conducted with thirty criminal trial court judges in Chicago, St. Louis, Milwaukee, and Indianapolis. These judges were questioned about their perceptions of female offenders in their courts, the way they responded to them in the determination of guilt or innocence, and whether they treated women differently than men at the time of sentencing.

On the preferential versus punitive debate, Simon (1975) noted the lack of long-term trend data, commenting that "these data allow us to see only that women as recently as 1972 seem to be receiving some preferential treatment at the bar of Justice" and that "the eyes of Justice are neither blinded nor fully opened, rather they seem to be open just enough to be able to discern the sex of the defendant and to allow that characteristic to influence the decision to some extent" (p. 67). The interviews with the judges supported the statistical data in that most of the judges said that they do not distinguish between defendants on the basis of sex when determining whether a defendant is guilty or innocent but that the defendant's sex does have some effect on their decisions concerning sentencing. Most said that they are more likely to treat women more leniently— that is, they are more inclined to recommend probation rather than imprisonment, and, if they do sentence a woman to prison, it is usually for a shorter time than a man who committed the same offense would have to serve.

In this book, we try to determine whether the increase in women's appearances in courts, as well as the increase in the seriousness of the crimes for which they are charged (we focus primarily on the property offenses), has resulted in a decrease in the differences between the percentages of men and women found guilty and in the sentences handed down to men and women.

Under the general rubric of equal rights, Simon (1975) noted the relative absence of vocational programs and industries in women's as opposed to men's prisons. A 1971 survey of female inmates in two of the three federal prisons found that 85 percent wanted more job training and 80 percent wanted more educational opportunities. Nine out of ten respondents said that they expected to work and support themselves when they were released. Drawing on an article titled "The Sexual Segregation of American Prisons," which appeared in the *Yale Law Journal* (vol. 82, no. 6), Simon reported:

> The average number of programs in the men's prisons is 10; in the female institutions the average number is 1.7. Whereas male prisoners have a choice of some fifty different vocational programs, the women's choices are limited to cosmetology (and in some states, convicted felons are forbidden by law to work in the field), clerical training, food services, serving, IBM key punching, and nurses' aides. Some of the men's prisons provide vocational training in programs that are available to women inmates as well; but none of the prisons for women are prepared to train their inmates in programs that are available for men.
>
> The industries available at men's and women's institutions that can provide a source of livelihood for the inmates show much the same picture. In the forty-seven prisons for men, there is an average of 3.2 industries as compared to 1.2 in the fifteen female prisons. There is also hardly any overlap concerning the types of industries in which both male and female inmates may work. (pp. 82–83)

In this book, we report the results of subsequent surveys, including one we conducted in 1989 of all the women's prisons in the country. We describe the vocational programs, industries, and academic programs that currently exist in women's prisons.

A second theme that is carried over from the first edition concerns female inmates as mothers of young children. As in the early 1970s, most women in prison today are mothers of young children. In the early 1970s, none of the women's prisons had any provisions for children, either for babies born to women while they were in prison or for their children when they came to visit. As part of our survey of vocational and academic programs, we asked the wardens about provisions and facilities that are currently available for infants and young children. Their responses appear in chapter 6.

To sum up, this second edition focuses on updating demographic data, which indicate changes in women's social status and involvement in criminal activities, both in the frequency of their participation and in the types of acts for which they are arrested. We examine court data to see whether there has been any change in judges' treatment of women at either the determination of guilt or sentencing stage. And we look at the changes in the opportunities women have to acquire academic and vocational skills and to earn money by working in prison industries, as well as the provisions and programs available for spending time with their children.

1

Women and Crime in Review

Four basic themes have dominated sociological discussions of the etiology of contemporary female criminality since the publication of the first edition of this book in 1975. These themes can be classified as (1) the masculinity thesis, (2) the opportunity thesis, (3) the economic marginalization thesis, and (4) the chivalry thesis. The first two themes often are grouped together under the title "liberation thesis," as both attempt to link changes in female crime with the improved status of women, which is viewed as a consequence of the contemporary women's movement. As we shall see, however, there are fundamental differences in the theoretical propositions of these two approaches. The third theme, economic marginalization, disputes the conclusions of the first two. The chivalry thesis questions whether observed increases in female crime are due to the increasing criminality of women or to an increasing willingness on the part of criminal justice personnel to apprehend, prosecute, and punish female offenders.

This chapter reviews these perspectives and broadly sketches relevant theoretical and empirical issues. We do not, however, attempt to catalog or detail the work of the many criminologists who have dealt with issues of women and crime over the past decade and a half.[1]

The Masculinity Thesis

The masculinity thesis was popularized by Freda Adler's *Sisters in Crime* (1975). This perspective is based on a *subjectivist* orientation that links changes in criminality to changes in subjective attitudes engendered by changes in the substantive nature of sex roles. This perspective predicts a causal nexus between the women's movement, changing social roles of women, the masculinization of female behavior (particularly a hypothetical change from passivity to aggressiveness as women assume male social roles), and changes in patterns of female offending.

Specifically, this thesis claims that as women are liberated and assume traditional male social roles, they begin to assert themselves in typically male ways—that is, they become aggressive, pushy, and hardheaded. Moreover, they learn to use crime as a shortcut to success and financial well-being and are more prone to use violence than in the past. The masculinization thesis predicts that to the extent that women's attitudes and behaviors become masculinized through their liberation and consequential assumption of traditional male social roles, their rates and patterns of criminal offending increasingly will approximate those of men. This change will be most evident in patterns of violent offending, which reflect the increasing aggressiveness of liberated women.

Adler's masculinity thesis is a sociological variant of the masculinity complex that Freud attributed to the "maladjusted woman" who, in reaction to penis envy, rebels against her natural inferiority. While not implying that liberated masculinized women are suffering from a psychological maladjustment, this thesis nevertheless focuses on the criminal potential of women who, in their rebellion against social inferiority, aggressively pursue masculine goals of success and power. While masculine qualities generally are viewed as positive ones for men to exhibit, proponents of the masculinization thesis join their Freudian counterparts in imputing a negative connotation to such characteristics in women (Deming 1977). Good girls are still those who maintain their allegiance to traditional social roles, while bad girls are those who act like men.

The masculinization thesis has been criticized from several different angles. Numerous studies have examined the relationship between criminal or delinquent behavior and role perceptions and attitudes, finding that the hypothesized relationship between either masculine traits or profeminist (liberated) attitudes and offending behavior is not supported empirically (Leventhal 1977; Norland and Shover 1978; Cernkovich and Giordano 1979; Thorton and James 1979; Widom 1979; Grasmick, Finley, and Glaser, 1984). As Naffine (1987) states, "Efforts to uncover the aggressively competitive nature of criminal women looking for their piece of the action or to find signs of feminism among female offenders have met with remarkably little success" (p. 104).

Perhaps most condemning of this perspective are criticisms based on analyses of actual arrest trends, which indicate that the hypothesized post–women's movement increases in violent and aggressive criminality among women are mythical (Simon 1975; Steffensmeier 1980a, 1980b, 1982; Leonard 1982; Box and Hale 1983; Feinman 1986; Weisheit and Mahan 1988).

The Opportunity Thesis

The opportunity thesis of female criminality originated in the first edition of this book, and its general propositions are espoused in this edition. This thesis argues that women are neither more or less moral than men, nor are they more or less inclined to engage in criminal acts. Rather, it assumes an *objectivist* orientation and argues that opportunities, skills, and social networks historically have contributed to men's propensity to commit crimes, while these same factors have limited women's opportunities. It is women's objective locations within the social structure and particularly within the occupational sphere, as well as in the private, family sphere, that influence the nature of their criminality.

Labor force participation is crucial to this argument. A wide range of property offenses can be committed only by persons who have access to other people's money and goods. Thus, crimes such as larceny, theft, embezzlement, and fraud are likely to be committed by persons who are in the labor force, not by full-time homemakers and mothers. The opportunity thesis also predicts a relationship between the positions that persons occupy in the labor force and their opportunities for committing various types of offenses. Executives, managers, and professionals such as accountants and attorneys have opportunities to embezzle much larger sums than do secretaries, bank tellers, and clerks. Thus, the argument goes, as more women enter the labor force and move into positions involving expert knowledge and skills, they will have more opportunities to commit the type of employment-related crimes committed by men. Some women will take advantage of these opportunities, just as some men do.

The opportunity thesis posits that as the employment patterns of men and women become more similar, so too will their patterns of employment-related crimes. To the extent that either the quantitative or qualitative labor force experiences of men and women remain dissimilar, so too should their rates and patterns of offending. Similarly, the rates and patterns of crimes committed by men and women outside the context of legitimate employment should be similar to the extent that the structured conditions of their lives resemble one another. Whether changes in labor force and other life conditions have placed men and women in structured social situations that resemble one another is an empirical question, as is the extent to which male and female criminality has changed.

As for violent acts, the argument advanced in the first edition claims that as women become more economically self-sufficient (a function of their increased education and labor force participation), they will be less likely to play the role of victim. As they become less beholden to men for their economic and social status, they will gain self-esteem and confidence. In turn, such women will be more likely to extricate themselves from situations of verbal and physical abuse before they reach a level of desperation at which only the death of the abusive person can release them from their torment.

Overall, the opportunity thesis claims that as women acquire more education, enter the labor force full-time, and assume positions of greater authority, prestige, and technical skills, they will use the opportunities available to them to commit white-collar property offenses in the same proportions as do their male counterparts. Also as a function of an improved socioeconomic status, they will move away from the role of victim and extricate themselves from situations that are likely to result in violent acts. Like the masculinity thesis, the opportunity thesis predicts that changes in the social status of women, which have resulted at least in part from the contemporary women's movement, will result in changes in the offending patterns of women. Unlike the masculinity thesis, the opportunity thesis predicts reduced rates of violent offending among women and increased rates of employment-related property offenses such as larceny/theft, embezzlement, fraud, and forgery. Just as men who commit such offenses need not be considered aggressive, neither should women who commit them.

What this perspective leaves out are the physical differences between men and women, which the women's movement has not changed. Most women are still at a disadvantage vis-à-vis men in personal, violent types of encounters, especially when the potential victim is awake and in control of his or her capacities. Robbery probably best illustrates the greater natural advantages that men have over women. The trends over time for robbery arrests show that it is one of the serious offenses in which women are least represented.

Women also differ from men in the skills they have acquired for carrying out certain types of offenses, as shown in their underrepresentation in male-dominated associations that involve organized crime, fence operations, and apprenticeship opportunities for skills such as safecracking. As long as women remain closed out of such opportunities, the types of offenses in which they engage will be limited.

Criticisms of the opportunity thesis have proliferated since the publication of the first edition of this book. In addition to the argument of theorists espousing the economic marginalization thesis, which is discussed in the next section, two other arguments remain central to the critique. The first is based on the claim that men and women, given the same structural opportunities, will behave differently. The second argument questions whether the improved status of women and/or an increase in their occupationally related crime rates are empirical realities.

To advance their position, supporters of the first argument begin with the observation that the stresses and strains of poverty and blocked opportunity structures, long hypothesized to cause criminality among lower-class males, have not resulted in similar rates and patterns of offending among lower-class females.

This gender-ratio problem, so termed by Daly and Chesney-Lind (1988), has obvious implications for all groups of similarly situated men and women. It logically follows that factors that normally drive men to commit white-collar crimes should not be expected to have a similar effect on women. Eileen Leonard (1982) summarizes this position as follows:

> The argument that increased white-collar employment for women will lead to increased white-collar crime among them assumes that women behave the same as men, given apparently similar situations. Yet, we should know that this is not so. The poverty, the unemployment, and the limited opportunities that supposedly drive men to commit crime, have not had the same effect on women. Perhaps the opportunity for white collar crime will not have the same effect on them either. . . . Given their vastly different historical, social, and economic experiences, women should not be expected to behave like men. Even in apparently similar situations, they will behave differently. (p. 182)

Exactly why this is so remains an unsettled topic of discussion. The rationales that have been advanced to explain why women and men have not behaved, and should not be expected to behave, in similar ways when structurally situated in similar economic situations generally stress differences in female socialization and/or social control. In essence, the idea is that women, regardless of where or whether they work, are more subject to internal and informal social controls than are men. From birth, they are oversocialized to be dependent, passive, self-sacrificing, and overcontrolled, restricted to the private sphere of home and family or limited in their freedom to assert themselves independently in the public sphere (Box 1983, Heidensohn 1985; Hagan, Gillis, and Simpson 1985; Messerschmidt 1986; Hagan, Simpson, and Gillis 1979).

In short, these arguments imply that objective structural conditions are possibly mediated by, or interact with, more fundamental patriarchal gender relationships, characterized by male domination at home and in the workplace, to create qualitatively different objective social realities and opportunities as well as different subjective situational definitions. Thus, the appearance of structural parity at any level of social status is just that—an appearance. The subordination of women conditions their reality within race, class, and status groupings, making it different from that of their male counterparts.

Proponents of this view do not deny that opportunity plays a large role in differentials between male and female offending patterns and rates. However, they wish to direct attention to differential processes of socialization and social control, which continue to structure both objective opportunities and subjective perceptions of them. Exception is taken to the notion that increased female labor force participation alone, or even the (disputable) existence of equal opportunity for women, indicates any measure of true liberation. Instead, the focus is on manifestations of male domination in the home, work, and society that constrain women's activity, both criminal and noncriminal.

The second argument against the assertions of the opportunity thesis, that neither the status of women nor their patterns of criminal offending has changed, is advanced by Steffensmeier (1980a, 1980b, 1982). Steffensmeier has been the most persistent and frequently cited opponent of the opportunity thesis and the masculinization thesis as well. While his analysis of arrest trends generally supports the prediction that the offending gap between males and females narrowed in the 1970s for the crimes of larceny and fraud and, to a lesser extent, embezzlement and forgery, his interpretation of the substantive meaning of these trends differs from the one offered by proponents of the opportunity thesis. Rather than viewing these rates as indicative of new opportunities for white-collar and/or employment-related criminal activity, Steffensmeier maintains that they simply reflect traditional sex role expectations, behaviors, and opportunities:

> The available research indicates that most arrests of women for larceny are for shoplifting and arrests for fraud involving passing "bad checks," credit card fraud, fraudulent theft of services, and small con games. Women are not being arrested for fraud which are occupationally related or which tend to be real white-collar crimes, such as false advertising, product defects and so on. Forgery is also a crime that is consistent with female sex roles and fits into the everyday round of activities in which women engage, especially since the skills and techniques required for forging credit cards, checks, etc., are learned in the normal process of growing up. It is the case that those arrested for forgery tend to be amateurs, or "naive forgers."
>
> Contrary to popular assumptions, the person arrested for embezzlement is usually more a petty thief than a white-collar offender. Most arrests for embezzlement are not persons of high social standing and responsibility who commit a crime in the course of their occupation and which involves large sums of money. Rather the typical embezzler is the trusted clerk, cashier or secretary who takes his or her employer's money and the amount taken is usually small. (Steffensmeier 1982, 124)

In essence, Steffensmeier (1982) does not dispute the theoretical assumptions underlying the opportunity thesis, only the empirical assertion that women have been able, as a result of the women's movement, to change their structural location in society and that such a change is related to changes in their commission of occupational crimes. He questions whether women actually have new labor force opportunities that would allow them opportunities qualitatively approaching those available to men. He maintains that the status of women is still lower than that of men and that women are still limited to traditionally female occupations providing opportunities for traditionally female crimes. Moreover, he suggests that access to illegitimate opportunities is even more limited to women than is access to legitimate opportunities. Criminal networks, within both the workplace and the criminal underworld, still discriminate on the basis of gender (Steffensmeier 1982 and Steffensmeier and Terry 1986).

Steffensmeier (1980a, 1980b) argues that a different kind of opportunity could be related to increases in larceny/theft (which he attributes to shoplifting). Self-service marketing and credit card sales provide increasing opportunities for petty thefts. These opportunities occur in an economic context that has forced the emancipation of many women, requiring them to support themselves and their families in traditionally female, low-paying jobs. Thus, he attributes increases in female property crime to the convergence of market consumption trends and the worsening economic conditions of women "rather than to women's liberation or changing sex roles" (Steffensmeier 1982, p. 126).

Steffensmeier's argument is consistent with the economic marginalization thesis. But before turning our attention to that theme, we need to look a bit more closely at the issue of white-collar criminality among women. Few studies have addressed this issue, and thus we know little about it. At present, we have no systematic evidence regarding the qualitative nature of contemporary women's white-collar offending relative to that of contemporary men. Have the men and women who represent the national statistics in the crime categories of larceny, forgery, fraud, and embezzlement been arrested for the same types of crimes, and are the reasons motivating these men and women similar? To date, only two studies—Daly (1989c) and Zietz (1981)—have tried to address the qualitative dimensions of this issue, but both are limited in their generalizability.

As Daly (1989c) points out, Zietz's (1981) study provides the most sustained inquiry into the nature of female offenders convicted of embezzlement, fraud, forgery, and theft. The purpose of Zietz's study was to compare her sample of women to the typologies of white-collar/property offenders developed from studying samples of male offenders, particularly Cressey's *Other People's Money* (1953), in order to determine whether these typologies are applicable to women. In short, she concludes that they are not. She finds that generally women are different in the vocabularies they use to justify their crimes, as well as in their motivations for committing criminal acts. In contrast to studies of men, Zietz found that for women, the violation of financial trust is often tied to an emotional relationship to others and the fulfillment of role expectations within that relationship—that is, the money gained is considered necessary to fulfill a caretaking role or to maintain a love relationship rather than to pay for personal excesses.

One could argue that even if Zietz's findings are generalizable, the differential motivations and justifications of male and female offenders do not obfuscate the reality that women's objective location in the occupational structure determines the opportunities they have to fulfill their perceived responsibilities through the violation of financial trust. If they were not in those occupational positions, they would not have access to the means that those positions provide. In short, their behaviors, in taking advantage of their structural opportunities to fulfill their needs, can be similar to the behaviors of similarly situated men, even if the motivational basis of their needs differs.

Thus, Zietz's study, while important and illuminating in its own right, provides little insight into the Simon-Steffensmeier disagreement, except to suggest that the gender structure of the public sphere of work may not be the only relevant issue (see Bartel 1979). Women's social status relative to men has at least two dimensions, and a change in one does not necessarily mean that there is a change in the other. Differentials in perceived role responsibilities in the private sphere of personal relationships may be just as important in explaining female criminality both within and outside of the workplace.

But what of the nature of white-collar crime? Are the offending behaviors of men and women similar? Daly (1989c) took the first serious qualitative look at gender differences in white-collar offending. Examining a group of federal offenders incarcerated for embezzlement, fraud, and forgery, she found the following:

1. The female share of corporate (or organizational) crime was low.

2. The female share of occupational crime was negligent for all crimes with the exception of bank embezzlement, in which the female share was close to 50 percent.

3. Generally, the women were more likely than the men to offend alone, outside the context of a crime group.

4. The offenses committed by the women involved less financial gain than those committed by the men.

5. The motives of the men and women differed in that the women cited family responsibilities more often than the men but not as much as Zietz's study suggested.

More interesting were the characteristics of Daly's sample, summarized as follows:

Men's white-collar crimes were both petty and major, but almost all the women's were petty. Although half or more of the employed men were managerial or professional workers, most employed women were clerical workers. Higher proportions of women were black and had no ties to the paid labor force; fewer women had a four-year college degree. The women's socioeconomic profile, coupled with the nature of their crimes, makes one wonder if "white-collar" aptly describes them or their illegalities. . . . [T]hese data suggest that if women's share of white-collar arrests increases, it will stem from (1) increasing numbers of women in highly monitored, money-changing types of clerical, sales, or service jobs, and (2) increasing numbers of poor or unemployed women attempting to defraud state and federal governments or banks by securing loans, credit cards, or benefits to which they are not legally entitled. (Daly 1989c, 790)

In conclusion, Daly (1989c) supports Steffensmeier's contention that the *Uniform Crime Report (UCR)* crime categories of fraud, forgery, and embezzlement are poor indicators of white-collar offenses, particularly for women. She also suggests a preference for the economic marginalization thesis over the opportunity thesis as an explanation for increasing crime among women.

The Economic Marginalization Thesis

The economic marginalization thesis is perhaps the most pervasive alternative to the opportunity thesis. This thesis posits that "it is the absence, rather than the availability, of employment opportunity for women [that] seems to lead to increases in female crime" (Naffine 1987, 98).[2] Proponents of this view take as their point of departure several related notions:

1. Greater participation in the labor force does not necessarily mean either more equality between the sexes or an improved economic situation for women.

2. The bulk of female offenders, if employed at all, are concentrated in a pink-collar ghetto, and their positions are characterized by poor pay and unrewarding, insecure work.

3. Female crime, the bulk of which is petty property crime, constitutes a rational response to poverty and economic insecurity.

(See Crites 1976; Klein and Kress 1976; Smart 1976 and 1979; Chapman 1980; Datesman and Scarpetti 1980; Gora 1982; Box and Hale 1983; Chesney-Lind 1986; Feinman 1986; Miller 1985; Messerschmidt 1986.)

Noting that the majority of female offenders are lower-class women who have committed non–employment-related crimes rather than middle- and upper-class professional women who have committed employment-related crimes, proponents of this theory suggest that feminization of poverty, not women's liberation, is the social trend most relevant to female criminality. They argue that in general, the economic pressures on women caused by unemployment, poorly paid employment, and/or inadequate welfare payments, combined with the increasing numbers of female-headed households supporting dependent children, lead more and more women to seek the benefits of criminal activity as supplements or alternatives to employment. In other words, economic necessity is forcing the emancipation of women from more law-abiding standards of conduct.

In short, advocates of the economic marginalization thesis support Steffensmeier's position and reject the idea that the majority of women have improved their social standing in the economic sphere relative to men. While these theorists do not deny observable increases in labor force participation among women, they contend that employment opportunities for women remain restricted, and thus the qualitative reality of the occupational distribution of women, while somewhat transformed over the years, remains substantially different from that of men. Occupational segregation concentrates women in lower-paying, less secure positions than those occupied by their male counterparts. The relevant implications of this concentration is neatly stated by Stallard, Ehrenreich, and Sklar (1983): "For men, poverty is often the consequence of unemployment, and a job is generally an effective remedy, while female poverty often exists even when a women works full-time" (p. 9).

In addition, it is argued that the stresses of female poverty often are exacerbated by the responsibilities of caring for dependent children. The disproportionately greater criminality of minority women, who also are disproportionately the heads of households with dependent children, is typically cited to support this assertion (Lewis 1981; Hagan 1985). To the extent that these theorists recognize small increases in employment-related crime, they attribute them to increased numbers of employed women who remain trapped in poverty rather than to increased numbers of upwardly mobile professional women.

Chesney-Lind (1986) summarizes the bases upon which theorists espousing the economic marginalization thesis refute the opportunity thesis:

> First, since women have not experienced major gains in the economic world, it seems implausible that any wave of female crime could be correctly laid at its door. . . . Second, studies of characteristics of female offenders showed that they bore no resemblance to the liberated "female crook" . . . but were instead minority women drawn from backgrounds of profound poverty who had committed "traditionally female" crimes such as petty theft or prostitution. (p. 81)

Feinman (1986), drawing on extensive experience with female offenders, is even more emphatic:

> Poverty and drugs are the major determinants of women's criminality. . . . [T]here is no evidence that could possibly link the women's movement either to the increase in crimes committed by women or to the nature of women's criminal behavior. They continue to act in traditional ways both in the crimes they commit and in the manner in which they commit them. . . .
>
> The women's movement has neither involved nor benefited the majority of women in the U.S. It has not even brought true equal opportunities for the minority of white middle and upper class women who have been most directly involved with the movement. Therefore, any discussion of the link between women's criminality and the women's movement is unrealistic. It only serves to perpetuate myths; it hinders efforts to learn the real causes of women's criminal behavior and to try to eliminate them. (p. 28)

A question that remains to be answered by the economic marginalization thesis is why women's selective criminal participation has continued to increase as women have moved into higher-status occupations. Female upward mobility into managerial, professional, and technical positions is demonstrated by the census data in chapter 3. The economic marginalization thesis would argue that as women move into more responsible positions, their propensities to commit property offenses will decline. The data show that the reverse has occurred. There is a positive relationship between female upward occupational mobility and higher female property, especially white-collar, arrest rates.

The Chivalry Thesis

The final theme running through much of the women and crime literature in the past fifteen years has been the issue of chivalry, or the more lenient treatment of female offenders by criminal justice personnel. In the first edition of this book, Simon (1975) speculates that a possible side effect of the women's liberation movement might be the decline of chivalry, or the encouragement of police and court personnel to treat women more like men, which presumably meant to arrest, convict, and sentence them to prison more often. This theme suggests that it has been a change in the official reaction to women's criminal behavior, rather than changes in that behavior itself, that accounts for increased numbers of women in official crime and prison statistics.

Simon (1975) suggests that women's call for equality in other realms of social, political, and economic life could invoke an unintended reaction in other realms such as criminal justice processing, creating an "if it's equality they want, it's equality they'll get" mentality among male police officers and court officials. Another expected effect of the women's movement on the reduction of chivalry toward female offenders was predicted to occur as more women entered the ranks of criminal justice practitioners, particularly as police officers. The logic of this argument was that female officers would be less likely to be conned into sympathy for female offenders.

The decline of chivalry as an explanation for increases in official rates of female criminality is based on the assumption that historically, chivalry did indeed operate to suppress official recognition of female criminality. This assumption has been challenged on the ground that any chivalry that might have benefited women has been selective chivalry at best. As Clarice Feinman (1986) explains, "Chivalry is reserved for white middle and upper class women, except those who flout culturally expected behavior for ladies" (p. 28).

The extent to which justice norms are based on gender has been the topic of considerable empirical inquiry within the criminological literature over the past decade and a half. With regard to police decision making, some empirical evidence suggests that over time, there has been a decline in chivalrous treatment of females at the stage of arrest (Krohn, Curry, and Nelson-Kilger 1983). However, the bulk of the research has been limited to contemporary cross-sectional analyses and suggests that where chivalry does exist, generalizations about such treatment must be made with considerable caution (DeFleur 1975; Chesney-Lind 1987; Visher 1983). Consistent with Feinman's assertion concerning chivalry are studies suggesting that not all women have been the recipients of lenient treatment by gallant police officers. Rather, only those women whose actions during their encounters with police are consistent with appropriate gender stereotypes have become the beneficiaries of chivalry.

After controlling for legal variables, Visher (1983) found that

> in encounters with police officers, those female suspects who violate typical middle-class standards of traditional characteristics and behaviors (i.e., white, older, and submissive) are not afforded any chivalrous treatment during arrest decisions. In these data, young, black, or hostile women receive no preferential treatment, whereas older, white women who are calm and deferential toward the police are granted leniency. (p. 23)

Whether this observed pattern of police encounters with female offenders has changed over the past decade, during which popular assumptions about both minority and women's equality have stabilized and during which the most significant increases in female (including minority female) representation on the police force have occurred, remains a largely unexplored issue.

In later criminal processing decisions, the evidence regarding the chivalrous treatment of women is ahistorical and mixed. Again, general statements must be viewed with caution. Women's treatment by the courts is reported in greater detail in chapter 5.

Factors other than a supposed decline in chivalry or paternalism on the part of individual police and court personnel must be considered when examining the effects of official reactions to female criminality as an explanation for the increased proportions of women in crime statistics. Changes in systematic factors such as surveillance and enforcement patterns, availability of correctional facilities and sentencing alternatives, and changes in reporting practices are the most obvious considerations. For example, if, as Steffensmeier (1982) contends, a large proportion of female larceny offenders have been arrested for shoplifting, increases in the female percentage of larceny arrests could be due to the increasing ability or willingness of retail establishments to pursue arrest and prosecution. Similarly, if, as Simon (1975) contends, increases in women's property offenses stem from occupational-related crimes, perhaps these increases could be attributable to a greater emphasis on white-collar crimes in recent years. Today large police departments commonly have special white-collar crime units that specialize in techniques appropriate for investigating such activity. Better investigatory practices may converge with the greater labor force participation of women to account for some of the observed increases in female property offending.

Conclusion

Contemporary theorists who have accepted the empirical assertion that there has been a rise in female criminality have attributed this phenomenon to one or a combination of historical social trends: (1) the psychological masculinization of women, (2) the increased labor force participation of women, (3) the feminization of poverty, and (4) less biased or more effective and efficient official responses to female criminality. Of these possible explanations, the masculinization thesis has proved the least satisfactory and has for the most part become an obligatory straw man in theoretical discussions of female criminality. Similarly, most contemporary theorists, regardless of their position on the decline of chivalry, would not assert that official reactions to female criminality have changed so drastically as to account for the bulk of observed changes in female criminality, particularly when measured by arrest statistics.

As stated earlier in this chapter, the opportunity thesis espoused in the first edition of this book also is espoused in this edition. But the fact that this perspective has caused considerable theoretical debate over the past fifteen years requires comment and qualification. While much effort has gone into discrediting the opportunity thesis, close examination reveals that it is still theoretically sound. Even proponents of the economic marginalization thesis do not argue against the notion that opportunities contribute to the nature of criminality. Instead, they dispute the following points:

1. The singularity of opportunity as a causal factor (What about differential stresses and strains and ways of perceiving them?)

2. The qualitative nature of women's opportunities (Is there actually increasing gender equality?)

3. The qualitative nature of women's crime (Is there an increase in women's white-collar offending or only in traditional female offending?)

4. The assumption that labor force equity (even if established empirically) suffices to create either objective or subjective social equality between the sexes (What about the interdependent effects of differential family responsibilities, gender role socialization, and informal social controls?)

If the opportunity thesis is recast, as it has been in this chapter, to focus on its prediction that men and women will behave in like manners when occupying similar positions in the social structure (that is, equally subject to the stresses generated by these positions and equally likely to take advantage of available legitimate and illegitimate opportunities that the positions present), discussions of this thesis can be more fruitful, particularly if we include position in family life as a codeterminant of social location. The first question for research becomes to what extent the social positions of men and women have become more similar, considering both their occupational positions and their family responsibilities. The second question is whether the offending behaviors of men and women have changed in a manner that is consistent with the relative changes in their social status vis-à-vis one another. We address these questions in chapters 3 and 4.

The most important question relative to theorizing about the relationship between social position, gender, and crime is this: Within similar social positions, are the offending behaviors of men and women similar to one another? This question cannot be examined using the existing national data. An analysis of this type would take into consideration what the research reported throughout this chapter suggests—namely, that theories about the "universal woman" neglect race/class differences among women and that the opportunity thesis and the economic marginalization thesis need not be mutually exclusive. Increasing numbers of upwardly mobile women may be committing white-collar crimes in the same proportions as similarly situated men at the same time that increasing numbers of their downwardly mobile sisters are committing the petty thievery, shoplifting, forgeries, and frauds that are available to them in their social positions. Conversely, each group of women may experience limitations on the availability of illegitimate opportunities (in the form of sexist exclusion, greater supervision and less independence, or differential socialization) relative to their male counterparts, but neither group can claim moral superiority.

Notes

1. Readers wishing such a review are directed to Leonard 1982; Mann 1984; Heidensohn 1985.
2. Proponents of the economic marginalization thesis vary widely in their theoretical orientations, from liberal feminist views concerned with the presence or absence of "discrimination" (Feinman 1986; Datesman and Scarpetti 1980; Chapman 1980) to more radical feminist perspectives concerned with the nature of power relations and their relationship to the gender, race, and class stratification of society (Smart 1976, 1979; Klein and Kress 1976; Messerschmidt 1986). For recent discussions of these different feminist perspectives, see Daly and Chesney-Lind 1988; Simpson 1989b.

2
The Contemporary Women's Movement

The contemporary women's movement was born in the late 1960s, a decade that saw the rise of a civil rights movement and a student-led antiwar movement. Many of those who participated in both these movements became leaders and organizers of various branches of the women's movement. In part, the experiences of younger women in the politics of the New Left served as the spawning ground for their desire to liberate themselves and their sisters. Women discovered that they were treated as second-class citizens even among men who were radical in many of their political and social beliefs, who believed in equality among the races, who advocated major changes in the occupational structure, and who favored redistribution of income and wealth. Women were expected to serve as bearers and servers and as bed companions to men in radical politics whose attitudes toward women did not differ significantly from those of men with more conservative views and life-styles.

Women who were active in the civil rights movement were struck especially by the similarities between their relationships with men and the relationships of blacks and whites. Using the language of the civil rights movement, women made analogies between a sex-caste system and a race-caste system; women were at the bottom of one system, and blacks were at the bottom of the other.

The array of women's movements in the sixties, from reform to revolutionary, reflected that of earlier movements in the period immediately preceding the Civil War and extending up through the 1920s. The National Women's Party (NWP), formerly the Congressional Union, was more militant than the National American Woman's Suffrage Association (NAWSA) and its successor, the League of Women Voters. Until the passage of the Nineteenth Amendment, both movements concentrated their efforts on the attainment of suffrage. But after 1920, the NWP devoted itself to the passage of an Equal Rights Amendment. In 1929, one year after suffrage had been attained, Alice Paul, leader of the NWP, minimized the value of the victory by stating, "Women today . . . are still in every way subordinate to men before the law, in the professions, in the church, in industry, and in the home" (Chafe 1972, 115).

Leaders of the NWP rejected attempts to form coalitions with other reform or progressive groups that were working for civil rights, disarmament, or improving the lot of the working people. Arguing in much the same vein as the radical women's movement of the 1970s, they reasoned that any expenditure of energy on issues that were extraneous to women's rights would only impede progress toward their major goal: freeing American women from their present condition of enslavement.

The NAWSA, under its new name, the League of Women Voters (LWV), pursued the opposite course. Its leaders contended that the attainment of suffrage had secured for them their most important and fundamental rights. They joined efforts with other groups for sound government, integrity in public life, and reforms in the economic and social spheres. The LWV went out of its way to avoid being identified as a lobby for only one group. Chafe (1972) quotes Dorothy Strauss, an LWV leader, as saying, "We of the League are very much for the rights of women, but we are not feminists primarily, we are citizens" (p. 115).

World War II brought an end both to conflict within the women's movement and to the women's movement per se (as it did to most other social reform movements). Not until two decades after the end of the war was the movement revived. And like the earlier movements, the contemporary women's movement followed on the heels of another social movement aimed at redressing the grievances of blacks and other ethnic minority groups. Whenever Americans became sensitive to the issue of human rights, it seemed, the women's movement acquired new support, and the 1960s was no exception to the rule. The civil rights movement did not cause the revival of feminism, but it did help to create a set of favorable circumstances (Chafe 1972, 233).

Catherine Stimpson (1971b) describes the historical ties that bound the black liberation and women's liberation movements together for more than a century. She points out that the antislavery movement preceded the first major women's rights movement, that black male suffrage preceded women's suffrage, and that the civil rights movement of the sixties preceded the contemporary women's liberation movement. Paraphrasing Alva Myrdal, she notes that both blacks and women are highly visible; they cannot hide even if they want to. A patriarchal ideology assigns them different qualities—blacks are tough; women are fragile—but both are judged to be naturally inferior in those respects that carry prestige, power, and advantages in society. Stimpson quotes Thomas Jefferson as follows:

> Even if America were a pure democracy, its inhabitants should keep women, slaves, and babies away from its deliberations. The less education women and Blacks get, the better; manual education is the most they can have. The

> only right they possess is the right which criminals, lunatics, and idiots share, to love their divine subordination within the *paterfamilias* and to obey the paterfamilias himself. (p. 623)

Women found that men with whom they had worked side by side against slavery or for civil rights, peace, or the right to organize in trade unions left them when they sought to gain the same rights for women. The behavior of Henry Stanton vis-à-vis his wife, Elizabeth, and the women's movement of that era is a case in point. The Stantons were both activists in the antislavery movement, but Henry left town when Elizabeth organized the women's rights convention in Seneca Falls in 1848.

Samuel Gompers and his successors, as heads of the American Federation of Labor (AFL), attacked the presence of married women in the work force and asserted that females should direct their energies toward getting married and raising families (Chafe 1972). In 1921, the Women's Trade Union League (WTUL) petitioned its executive council to issue federal charters that would permit women to organize in sexually segregated unions. The AFL rejected the petition, and when the women accused the executive council of prejudice, Gompers replied that the AFL discriminated against "any nonassimilable race" (Chafe 1972, 78). During World War II, R.J. Thomas, president of the United Auto Workers, claimed that women accepted the advantages of union membership but not the responsibilities. He predicted that at the end of the war, almost all women would lose their jobs.

The most recent feminists found that they received little interest, attention, or sympathy when they tried to have the discrimination they experienced recognized as a legitimate source of complaint:

> Like their ancestors in the antislavery movement, some women in the civil rights movement felt abused. They were given work supportive in nature and negligible in influence; they were relegated to the research library and to the mimeograph machine. . . . Not only did movement men tend to be personally chauvinistic, but many of the movement's ideals—strength, courage, spirit— were those society attributes to masculinity. Women may have those characteristics but never more than men. (Stimpson 1971b, 646)

And Stokely Carmichael, one of the leaders of the civil rights movement, remarked: "The only position for women in SNCC [Student Nonviolent Coordinating Committee] is prone" (Freeman 1975, 450).

In tracing the founding of the contemporary women's movement, Freeman (1973) cites an incident that she claims precipitated the formation of the Chicago group, the first independent women's group in the country:

At the August 1967 convention of the National Conference for New Politics, a women's caucus had met for days only to be told by the chair that its resolution wasn't significant enough to merit a floor discussion. Only by threatening to tie up the convention with procedural motions, did the women succeed in having their statement tacked on to the end of the agenda. But in the end, their resolution was never discussed. The chair refused to recognize any of the many women standing by the microphones. Instead he recognized someone from the floor to speak on the "forgotten American, the American Indian." Five women rushed to the podium and demanded an explanation. The Chairman responded by patting one of them on the head (literally) and saying, "Cool down, little girl. We have more important things to talk about than women's problems. (pp. 800–801)

Another incident that illustrates the lack of empathy that men in the radical politics of the sixties had for women's rights occurred at the University of Washington. A Students for a Democratic Society (SDS) organizer was explaining to a large meeting how white college youths established rapport with the poor whites with whom they were working. He said that sometimes, after analyzing societal ills, the men shared leisure time by "balling a chick together." He pointed out that such activities did much to enhance the political consciousness of the poor white youths. A woman in the audience asked, "And what did it do for the consciousness of the chick?" After the meeting, a handful of enraged women formed Seattle's first women's group (Freeman 1973, 801).

Women's liberation groups continue to see connections between their status in American society and the status of blacks. In comparing the ideology of the women's movement with that of black civil rights advocates, Stimpson (1971b) observes, "[The black movement] teaches that the oppressed must become conscious of their oppression, of the debasing folly of their lives, before change can come. Change, if it does come, will overthrow both a class, a social group, and a caste—a social group held in contempt" (p. 648).

Stimpson goes on to make perhaps the strongest statement of the contemporary women's movement on the similarities between themselves and blacks:

1. Women, like black slaves, belong to a master. They are property and whatever credit they gain redounds to him.
2. Women, like black slaves, have a personal relationship to the men who are their masters.
3. Women, like blacks, get their identity and status from white men.
4. Women, like blacks, play an idiot role in the theatre of the white man's fantasies. Though inferior and dumb, they are happy, especially when they can join a mixed group where they can mingle with The Man.
5. Women, like blacks, buttress the white man's ego. Needing such support,

the white man fears its loss; fearing such loss, he fears women and blacks.

6. Women, like blacks, sustain the white man: "They wipe his ass and breast feed him when he is little, they school him in his youthful years, do his clerical work and raise him and his replacements later, and all through his life in the factories, on the migrant farms, in the restaurants, hospitals, offices, and homes, they sew for him, stoop for him, cook for him, clean for him, sweep, run errands, haul away his garbage, and nurse him when his frail body falters."

7. Women, like blacks, are badly educated. In school they internalize a sense of being inferior, shoddy, and intellectually crippled. In general, the cultural apparatus—the profession of history, for example—ignores them.

8. Women, like blacks, see a Tom image of themselves in the mass media.

9. Striving women, like bourgeois blacks, become imitative, ingratiating, and materialistic when they try to make it in the white man's world.

10. Women, like blacks, suffer from the absence of any serious study on the possibility of real "temperamental and cognitive differences" between the races and sexes. (p. 649)

Since the end of the 1960s, many variations of the initial women's movement have emerged. These movements and ideologies range from reformist to revolutionary. The National Organization for Women (NOW) is probably the most conservative. Maintaining the civil rights analogy, it is the National Association for the Advancement of Colored People (NAACP) of the women's movement. Founded in 1966 by Betty Friedan, it has concentrated most of its efforts on legal and economic problems. Its membership is, on the average, older than that of the more radical women's groups, but like the more radical groups, it is composed primarily of white, well-educated professional women.

Between the end of the sixties and the early part of the seventies, a variety of women who became disenchanted with, or were thrown out of, New Left or civil rights movements organized Female Liberation First (FLF), Women's International Terrorist Conspiracy from Hell (WITCH), Red Stockings, and the Feminists. The characteristics that distinguish the moderate groups from the more radical ones are the almost exclusive emphasis that the former place on job equality and passage of the Equal Rights Amendment; the strategy of working for change within the system through lobbying, court action, and education; and the willingness to accept men as members. The radical groups consider the entire system corrupt. Their targets are as much the institutions of marriage, the family, and motherhood as unequal opportunities in employment and education. Consciousness raising for these women involves educating their sisters to the belief that every aspect of their relationship with men is exploitive. The "Red Stocking Manifesto" expresses those sentiments:

Women are an oppressed class. Our oppression is total, affecting every facet of our lives. We are exploited as sex objects, domestic servants, and cheap labor. We are considered inferior beings, whose only purpose is to enhance men's lives. Our humanity is denied. Our prescribed behavior is enforced by the threat of physical violence.

Because we have lived so intimately with our oppressors in isolation from each other, we have been kept from seeing our personal suffering as a political condition. This creates the illusion that a woman's relationship with her man is a matter of interplay between two unique personalities and can be worked out individually. In reality, every such relationship is a class relationship, the conflicts between individual men and women are political conflicts that can only be solved collectively.

We identify the agents of our oppressors as men. Male supremacy is the oldest, most basic form of domination. All other forms of exploitation and oppression (racism, capitalism, imperialism, etc.) are extensions of male supremacy: men dominate women; a few men dominate the rest.

We identify with all women. We define our best interest as that of the poorest, most brutally exploited women. We repudiate all economic, racial, education, or status privileges that divide us from other women. (Epstein and Goode 1973, 178)

Some women's groups espouse homosexual relationships as a desirable alternative to heterosexual ones. The Feminists, for example, argue that the basic assumption of most women's groups that women's lives will always be intertwined with men's ignores an important option: Women might consider living separately from men and accepting homosexual relations as an alternative to heterosexual relationships.

Abbott and Love (1971) write:

Recognition of the validity of the lesbian lifestyle and acceptance of lesbian activism in women's liberation is crucial to the women's movement's ultimate goal—a new, harmonious, cooperating, nonauthoritarian society in which men and women are free to be themselves. To end the oppression of the lesbian is to admit of a wider range of being and acting under the generic name "woman." It is a cause that must be undertaken by women's liberation if women are truly to free themselves. (p. 621)

For all the ideological differences and tactical variations that exist within the women's movement, the demographic characteristics of the various groups' membership are extraordinarily homogeneous. In the main, the movement is led by, appeals to, and has as the large majority of its members young white women who are college educated and whose families are middle and upper-middle class. After they leave the university, most of these women enter professions. None of the groups within the movement has substantially incorporated into its ranks blue-collar workers, black women, or high school–educated married women. The gulf between these nonmovement women and the authors of the "Red Stocking Manifesto" may be as great as any that those writers envisage between men and women.

It is still too early to tell how likely it is that the women's movement will significantly alter the behaviors, perceptions, beliefs, and life-styles of women already involved in criminal careers. But given the characteristics of the members of the women's movement, it is unlikely that it has had a significant impact or that it has made much of an impression on women already involved in crime. Indeed, most of those women have yet to hear of consciousness raising or of sisterhood in a political sense. Those who have may well ridicule those sentiments or attack them as the empty mouthings of women whose lives have always been characterized by material comfort, stability, and security.

Kate Millett's (1973) observations of how prostitutes behave in court dramatizes the point:

> The scene in court is astonishing: the woman is absolutely flirting throughout the whole proceedings. She does it when she comes in, she does it when she's going out with the cops and clerks. It doesn't break down for a minute. That interchange is very weird to watch and it's something that would take a long time to explain, but you know the woman's security and advantage lies in maintaining the relationship. (p. 157)

There is one avenue, however, through which the women's movement may already be having a significant impact on women in crime. The movement's rhetoric and activities may alter the treatment that women offenders receive at the hands of the police, prosecutors, and other law enforcement personnel. What we have heard from many police officers is "If it's equality these women want, we'll see that they get it."

A Brief Update

In 1990, we find the women's movement dominated by NOW. The issues that consume most of women's energies are abortion, child care, comparable worth, and other work-related matters such as sexual harassment and the development of strategies for the appointment and election of women to public office and important government positions.

In 1967, NOW had 700 members in 14 chapters. In 1971, it had between 5,000 and 10,000 members who belonged to 150 chapters. In 1974, there were 40,000 members and 1,000 chapters. In 1977, NOW reported a membership of 60,000; in 1981, it grew to 150,000; and in 1983, it was 175,000. The expanding membership introduced more heterogeneity into the organization. In recent years, much of NOW's growth has come from lower-level white-collar workers and housewives. Yet in 1974, NOW elected Aileen Fernandez, a black woman, as president. Fernandez told her constituents, "Some black sisters are not sure that the feminist movement will meet their current needs." (NOW 1974)

In the 1980s, NOW became the major umbrella organization for women's interests. Two relatively new groups, the National Abortion Rights League (NARAL) and the National Political Caucus, also have gained in membership and support. The former is a one-issue organization; the latter aims to attract more women to run for public office.

As the last decade of the twentieth century opens, the women's movement that began in the 1960s has grown and become more diversified in its membership as well as in the issues it espouses. The fear that the movement might focus all of its energies on one issue, the passage of the Equal Rights Amendment (ERA), did not materialize. While such an amendment is still an important item on the agenda of the contemporary women's movement, members of the movement may have learned some lessons from their predecessors and not allowed the success or failure of one issue to define the movement's reason for being.

In addition, during the 1980s, comparisons of men's and women's views on both women's issues (such as the ERA, abortion, and workplace issues) and on broader public policy questions revealed no significant differences. Men were no less likely to support the ERA or to assume a pro-choice position on abortion, for example, than were women. Analyses of how women and men reported having voted in presidential elections since the 1950s likewise revealed no significant gender differences. (Simon and Landis 1989).

The woman's movement is still alive and appears to be growing in both membership and scope. Groups that two or three decades ago advocated and predicted the demise of the nuclear family and that viewed marriage and motherhood as institutions that are inherently exploitive of women seem to have receded into the background. The sentiments expressed in the "Red Stocking Manifesto" are barely heard or listened to today, as women tend to view themselves less as victims and more as advocates of causes that will benefit them in particular and society in general.

3
American Women: Their Demographic and Status Characteristics

In this chapter, we examine census and other demographic data in order to update trends concerning marriage and divorce, fertility, education, and labor force participation among American women. We then assess how these factors are likely to influence women's participation in crime.

One thing we look at is whether increased participation in the labor force provides women with more opportunities for committing certain types of crimes. As those opportunities increase, women's participation in larceny, fraud, embezzlement, and other property and white-collar crime also should increase. As women enter the labor force in greater proportions, however, and as they acquire more skills through educational and occupation training, and they receive more generous financial compensation, their sense of frustration, feelings of being victimized, and sense of powerlessness should diminish. According to Ward, et al. (1968), Reckless and Kay (1967), and others who have studied women who have committed crimes of violence, it is these emotions that stimulate women to violence. The full set of expectations, then, is that women's participation in property and white-collar offenses should increase and their participation in crimes of violence should decrease as they gain greater entry into the work force and are rewarded for their contributions.

Demographic Trends

The 1987 Population Survey reported that there were 124,928 million women and 118,967 million men in the United States. Thus, women outnumbered men by almost 6 million. Among the fifteen-year-old or older population, women outnumbered men by some 7.5 million.

The percentages of unmarried women in specific age categories from 1950 to 1983 are shown in table 3–1. For all age categories and both races, there was an increase in the percentage of never-married women from 17.3 percent to 22.9 percent. Among white women thirty-five years old or older, the percentage of those who never married declined continuously from 1950 through 1983. But among black women, the percentage who never married increased during the same time period. The trends for black and white men paralleled those for black and white women.

Table 3–2 shows that between 1970 and 1986, the percentage of persons who had been divorced increased almost threefold and that increases were

Table 3–1
Percentage of Americans Who Never Married: 1950–1983

Age (years)	Women					Men				
	1950	1960	1970	1980	1983	1950	1960	1970	1980	1983
All races										
15–19 years	82.9	83.9	88.1	91.2	93.4	96.7	96.1	95.9	97.2	98.1
20–24 years	32.2	28.4	36.3	51.2	55.5	59.0	53.1	55.5	68.2	73.2
25–29 years	13.3	10.5	12.2	21.6	24.8	23.8	20.8	19.6	32.1	38.2
30–34 years	9.3	6.9	7.4	10.6	13.0	13.2	11.9	10.7	14.9	19.6
35 +	8.2	7.2	6.5	5.7	5.2	8.8	7.8	7.1	6.3	6.1
Total	18.5	17.3	20.6	22.9	22.9	24.9	23.2	26.4	29.7	30.0
White										
15–19 years	83.5	83.9	88.0	90.7	92.8	96.8	96.1	95.9	97.2	97.9
20–24 years	32.4	27.4	35.1	48.6	52.2	59.5	52.6	54.9	66.9	71.1
25–29 years	13.1	9.8	10.8	19.2	21.8	23.6	20.0	18.7	30.5	35.5
30–34 years	9.3	6.6	6.7	9.1	10.9	13.1	11.3	10.0	13.8	18.3
35 +	8.5	7.4	6.4	5.3	4.8	8.9	7.6	6.8	5.8	5.8
Total	18.5	17.0	19.9	21.2	21.1	24.7	22.6	25.6	28.0	28.4
Black[a]										
15–19 years	78.9	83.8	88.6	95.1	96.9	95.6	96.2	95.5	99.6	99.6
20–24 years	31.2	35.4	43.6	67.5	75.3	54.7	57.1	58.4	85.2	85.2
25–29 years	14.1	15.7	21.3	37.0	42.6	25.2	27.6	25.4	56.6	56.6
30–34 years	8.9	9.6	12.8	21.5	27.2	14.4	17.2	16.1	29.3	29.3
35 +	5.2	6.1	7.1	8.4	9.0	7.9	9.5	9.5	8.8	8.8
Total	18.8	20.0	26.2	34.1	36.0	26.6	28.3	32.9	40.6	42.4

Source: Bianchi and Spain 1986, p. 12, table 1.1. Data are from the U.S. Bureau of the Census, Census of Population: 1950, vol. 2, pt. 1, U.S. Summary, table 104; Census of Population; 1960, vol. 1, pt. 1, U.S. Summary, table 176; Census of Population: 1970, vol. 1, U.S. Summary, table 203; Census of Population 1980, vol. 1, chap. D, U.S. Summary, table 264. "Marital Status and Living Arrangements March 1983," Current Population series p-20, no. 389, table 1.

Note: Data for 1983 are from the Current Population Survey and are not strictly comparable to census data for earlier years.

[a]Data for 1950 and 1960 are for non-whites.

Table 3–2
Prevalence of Divorce among Black and White Women and Men:
1970–1986

	Women			Men		
	1970	*1980*	*1986*	*1970*	*1980*	*1986*
All races						
Total ever married (thousands)	34,299	36,169	43,111	31,304	35,326	38,912
Percent divorced	5.2	11.0	13.9	3.3	8.2	10.7
White						
Total ever married (thousands)	30,401	34,093	37,212	28,189	31,422	34,205
Percent divorced	5.0	10.5	13.4	3.1	7.9	10.7
Black						
Total ever married (thousands)	3,505	4,066	4,412	2,817	3,062	3,520
Percent divorced	7.7	16.5	20.7	5.5	12.6	13.2

Source: U.S. Bureau of the Census, *Statistical Abstract of the U.S.* (Washington, D.C.: U.S. Government Printing Office, 1988), p. 40, table 52.
Note: Figures represent "ever-married persons 25–45 years old who were divorced at the time of the survey." The 1986 figures are as of March 1986.

greater for black women than for white women. Both white and black women were more likely to have been divorced than were white and black men.

Trends in the overall percentage of ever-married women who remained childless show that between 1940 and 1960, a higher percentage of them were black but in 1970 and 1980, a higher percentage of white women remained childless (table 3–3). Overall, in 1980 21.2 percent of all ever-married white women fifteen years old or older remained childless, compared to 13.3 percent for all ever-married black women. For white women, the percentage increased between 1960 and 1980; for black women, it decreased.

As of 1980, there were some 80 million households in the United States, 73.3 percent of which were family households. Of these family households, 10.5 percent were headed by a woman, and 58 percent of them contained children. The data in table 3–4 show that in 1980, 46.5 percent of the mothers in those households had been divorced and 16.7 percent had never married. Those percentages represent big increases over the previous two decades, in which a much higher percentage of the women in female-headed households were widows.

To sum up, the demographic data tell us that from 1970 on, women delayed marriage longer than they did in the previous two decades and that the divorce rate increased between 1970 and 1986. The percentage of ever-married white women who remained childless went up between 1960 and 1980. For black women, the percentage went down. Among family households in 1980, 10.5 percent were headed by women, most of whom had been divorced or had never married. Fifty-eight percent of those households contained children.

Table 3–3
Percentage of Ever-Married Women Who Were Childless:
1940–1980

	Age						
	15–19	20–24	25–29	30–34	35–39	40–44	Total
All races							
1940	54.6	39.9	30.1	23.3	19.9	17.4	26.5
1950	52.8	33.3	21.1	17.3	19.1	20.0	22.8
1960	43.6	24.2	12.6	10.4	11.1	14.1	15.0
1970	50.9	35.7	15.8	8.3	7.3	8.6	16.4
1980	52.5	41.9	27.3	14.4	8.8	7.1	20.2
White							
1940	56.4	40.3	29.7	22.3	18.9	16.7	25.9
1950	55.4	34.0	20.1	15.8	17.5	18.9	21.8
1960	46.0	25.0	12.3	9.7	10.2	13.0	14.6
1970	53.7	37.5	16.1	8.1	6.9	8.1	16.7
1980	54.4	44.5	29.2	15.0	8.9	6.9	21.2
Black							
1940	46.6	38.7	35.1	31.0	28.8	25.8	32.8
1950	38.0	28.9	30.0	30.8	32.3	30.1	30.8
1960	25.3	17.0	14.2	15.8	20.0	24.7	18.7
1970	32.2	20.7	12.6	9.4	9.8	13.0	13.8
1980	40.2	24.4	15.3	10.3	8.7	8.5	13.3

Source: Bianchi and Spain 1986, p. 66, table 2.3. Data are from the U.S. Bureau of the Census, *Historical Statistics of the United States: Colonial Times to 1970*, Bicentennial Edition (Washington, D.C.: U.S. Government Printing Office, 1975), series B49–66; Census of Population: 1980, vol. 1, chap. D, U.S. Summary, table 270.

Table 3–4
Distribution of Female Heads of Households with Children:
1960–1980

Marital Status	Number (thousands)			Percent Distribution			1960–1980 Change	
	1960	1970	1980	1960	1970	1980	Number	Percent
Separated	454	767	1,047	24.0	25.4	21.2	280	61.7
Spouse absent	253	251	171	13.4	8.3	3.5	(80)	−31.6
Widowed	606	748	593	32.0	24.8	12.0	(155)	−25.6
Divorced	496	991	2,295	26.2	32.8	46.5	1,304	262.9
Never married	83	260	826	4.4	8.6	16.7	566	681.9
Total	1,892	3,017	4,932	100.0	100.0	100.0	1,915	101.2

Source: Bianchi and Spain 1986, p. 104, table 3.4. Data are from the U.S. Bureau of the Census, Census of Population: 1960, vol. 2, "Families," PC(2)-4A, tables 5 and 6; Census of Population: 1970, vol. 2.2, "Family Composition," PC(2)-4A, tables 6 and 8; Census of Population: 1980, vol. 1, chap. D, U.S. Summary, tables 267 and 268.

Women in the Labor Force

Between 1970 and 1987, the percentage of all women in the labor force increased from 42.6 to 55.4 percent. Table 3–5 indicates that the biggest increase in labor force participation occurred among married women, from 41 to 56 percent, in contrast to women in the single and widowed/divorced categories.

Among the married women, there were big increases in labor force participation among those with young children (table 3–6). In 1987, almost 57 percent of mothers with children under six years of age were in the labor force full-time.

The more years of schooling a woman had, the more likely she was to be in the labor force on a year-round, full-time basis. As shown in table 3–7, in 1980 more than 30 percent of the women with some college education worked full-time year-round, and 70 percent of the women with some college education were in the labor force, compared to 30 percent of the high school dropouts.

In the first edition of this book, Simon (1975) reported that women's participation in the labor force was based on a sex role definition that "has women performing in service-like roles and in jobs that involve less initiative and responsibility than those occupied by men" (p. 22). In comparing labor force participation across the four broad categories (white-collar, blue-collar, service, and farm), she noted that from 1948 through 1971, the proportion of women in the white-collar category increased from 49.3 to 61.1 percent and the proportion of women in service positions increased from 20.5 to 22.3 percent. In 1971, 34 percent of the women within the white-collar category held clerical positions, compared to 7 percent of the men, and 14.5 percent of the men held managerial positions, as opposed to 4.9 percent of the women (Simon 1975:24, Table 3–4).

Looking at the data in table 3–8, we see that in 1986, 9.8 percent of employed white women held executive/managerial positions, compared to 7.8 percent in 1980 and 4.0 percent in 1970. Overall, 27.9 percent of employed white women held managerial, professional, or technical positions in 1986, compared to 25.5 percent in 1980 and 19.8 percent in 1970. Among black women, the changes were smaller, increasing from 14 percent in 1970 to 19.8 percent in 1980 to 20.4 percent in 1986. The presence of white women in administrative support (clerical-like) positions declined between 1970 and 1986 from 34 to 30.1 percent, while the presence of black women increased from 19.2 to 26.1. For black women, the greatest change occurred between 1970 and 1980 in the private household (domestic) area, as their presence decreased from 17.8 percent in 1970 to 5 percent in 1980 to 4 percent in 1986. In summary, the data in table 3–8 show that women have moved upward from service and administrative positions to managerial, professional, and technical positions.

Table 3–5
*Females in the Labor Force as a Percentage of All Females by
Marital Status: 1940–1987*

	Single	Married	Widowed/Divorced	Total
1940	48.1	16.7	32.0	27.4
1944	58.6	25.6	35.7	35.0
1947	51.2	21.4	34.6	29.8
1950	50.5	24.8	36.0	31.4
1955	46.4	29.4	36.0	33.5
1956	46.4	30.2	36.9	34.2
1957	46.8	30.8	37.9	34.8
1958	45.4	31.4	37.9	35.0
1959	43.4	32.3	38.0	35.2
1960	44.1	31.7	37.1	34.8
1961	44.4	34.0	39.0	36.8
1962	41.7	33.7	36.6	35.7
1963	41.0	34.6	35.8	36.1
1964	40.9	34.4	36.1	36.5
1965	40.5	35.7	35.7	36.7
1966	40.8	35.4	36.4	37.3
1967	50.7	37.8	35.9	39.7
1968	51.3	38.3	35.8	40.7
1969	51.2	39.6	35.8	41.6
1970	53.0	41.4	36.2	42.6
1971	52.8	41.4	35.7	42.5
1972	55.0	42.2	37.2	43.7
1973	55.9	42.8	36.7	44.2
1974	57.4	43.8	37.8	45.3
1975	57.0	45.1	37.7	46.0
1976	59.2	45.8	37.3	46.8
1977	59.2	47.2	39.0	48.0
1978	60.7	48.1	39.9	49.2
1979	62.9	49.9	40.0	50.8
1980	61.5	50.7	41.0	51.1
1981	62.3	51.7	41.9	52.0
1982	62.2	51.8	42.1	52.1
1983	62.6	52.3	41.2	52.3
1984	63.1	53.3	42.1	53.2
1985	65.2	54.7	42.8	54.5
1986	65.3	55.0	43.1	54.7
1987	65.1	56.1	42.9	55.4

Source: U.S. Bureau of the Census, *Statistical Abstract of the U.S.* (Washington, D.C.: U.S. Government Printing Office, 1988), p. 374, table 623.

Table 3–6
Labor Force Participation Rates of Married Women with Children:
1948–1987[a]

	No Children under 18	Children 6–17; None under 6	Children under 6	Total
1948	28.4	26.0	10.8	22.0
1949	28.7	27.3	11.0	22.5
1950	30.3	28.3	11.9	23.8
1951	31.0	30.3	14.0	25.2
1952	30.9	31.1	13.9	25.3
1953	31.2	32.2	15.5	26.3
1954	31.6	33.2	14.9	26.6
1955	32.7	34.7	16.2	27.7
1956	35.3	36.4	15.9	29.0
1957	35.6	36.6	17.0	29.6
1958	35.4	37.6	18.2	30.2
1959	35.2	39.8	18.7	30.9
1960[b]	34.7	39.0	18.6	30.5
1961	37.3	41.7	20.0	32.7
1962	36.1	41.8	21.3	32.7
1963	37.3	41.5	22.5	33.7
1964	37.8	43.0	22.7	34.4
1965	38.3	42.7	23.3	34.7
1966	38.4	43.7	24.2	35.4
1967	38.9	45.0	26.5	36.8
1968	40.1	46.9	27.6	38.3
1969	41.0	48.6	28.5	39.6
1970	42.2	49.2	30.3	40.8
1980	46.0	61.7	45.1	50.1
1982	46.2	63.2	48.7	51.2
1983	46.6	63.8	49.9	51.8
1984	47.2	65.4	51.8	52.8
1985	48.2	67.8	53.4	54.2
1986	48.2	68.4	53.8	54.6
1987	48.4	70.6	56.8	55.8

Source: U.S. Bureau of the Census, *Historical Statistics of the United States: Colonial Times to 1970,* Bicentennial Edition (Washington, D.C.: U.S. Government Printing Office, 1975), series D63–84, table D63–74; U.S. Bureau of the Census, *Statistical Abstract of the U.S.* (Washington, D.C.: U.S. Government Printing Office, 1988), p. 374, table 624.

[a]Married women in the labor force as percent of married women in the population.
[b]First year for which figures include Alaska and Hawaii.

Table 3–7
*Labor Force Participation Rates of Women by Educational
Attainment: 1960–1980*

	In Labor Force			Worked Preceding Year			Worked Full-Time Year-Round		
	1960	1970	1980	1960	1970	1980	1960	1970	1980
Age ≥ 25 years									
Not high school graduate	30.8	33.3	30.8	36.1	38.5	33.5	12.0	13.1	12.4
High school, 4 years	39.1	46.7	53.6	45.1	52.9	57.9	19.5	21.9	26.6
College									
1–3 years	40.9	44.8	58.8	47.5	51.9	64.0	18.0	20.4	29.6
4 years	47.7	50.0	62.3	53.9	58.4	68.0	15.8	15.4	27.0
≥5 years	66.6	66.0	72.7	71.8	73.0	77.9	19.7	21.7	26.5
Total	35.3	40.8	48.4	41.0	46.9	52.5	14.9	17.3	22.3
Age = 25–34 years									
Not high school graduate	33.2	39.3	48.6	41.6	47.3	53.2	10.7	12.5	16.8
High school, 4 years	34.3	44.4	61.7	42.9	54.0	68.0	15.7	18.2	28.9
College									
1–3 years	35.5	46.4	69.5	46.2	57.5	76.3	14.6	20.4	34.6
4 years	41.6	53.4	74.8	52.5	66.2	81.3	14.6	14.9	35.0
≥5 years	58.6	70.6	79.6	67.4	79.0	86.7	17.6	21.9	30.3
Total	34.8	44.9	64.5	43.7	54.5	70.8	13.6	16.6	29.2

Source: Bianchi and Spain 1986, p. 131, table 4.7. Data are from U.S. Bureau of the Census, 1960, 1970, and 1980 Census 1/1,000 Public Use Microdata Sample.

Education

Between 1950 and 1985, the percentage of women who earned bachelor's degrees increased from 23.9 to 49.4 percent (table 3–9). In 1950, only 29.3 percent of the master's degrees were earned by women, but by the 1980s, women were receiving half of the degrees conferred. Women still lagged far behind men at the doctoral level, however. Roughly one-third of the recipients of doctorate degrees were women in the early 1980s, which is a big increase from the 9 percent of the 1950s but is clearly less than women's representation in the population.

Table 3–10 shows that while there were big increases in the percentage of women who were awarded professional degrees, men still dominated. Of the four major professions, women made the biggest inroads in law and medicine.

Table 3-8
Occupational Distribution by Race and Sex: 1970–1986[a]

| | Men | | | | | | Women | | | | | |
| | Blacks | | | Whites | | | Blacks | | | Whites | | |
	1970	1980	1986	1970	1980	1986	1970	1980	1986	1970	1980	1986
Managerial, professional, and technical												
Executive, administrative, managerial	2.9	5.7	6.7	10.8	13.5	14.1	1.7	4.7	5.9	4.0	7.8	9.8
Professional specialty	4.3	5.9	6.3	10.6	11.5	12.2	9.8	11.8	10.8	13.7	14.6	14.9
Technicians and related support	1.1	2.0	1.7	2.6	3.1	2.9	2.5	3.3	3.7	2.1	3.1	3.2
Total	8.3	13.6	14.7	24.0	28.1	29.2	14.0	19.8	20.4	19.8	25.5	27.9
Sales	2.9	3.9	5.2	10.4	9.8	11.9	4.4	6.1	8.7	11.8	12.0	13.6
Administrative support	7.8	9.3	9.1	7.2	6.6	5.4	19.2	25.9	26.1	34.0	32.1	30.1
Service												
Private household	0.5	0.2	0.1	0.1	0.1	0.1	17.8	5.0	4.0	2.0	0.8	1.7
Protective service	1.8	3.1	4.2	2.1	2.3	2.4	0.3	0.7	0.7	0.2	0.4	0.4
Other service	14.0	13.6	13.0	5.3	5.9	6.1	23.8	23.6	23.8	14.9	15.1	15.1
Total	16.3	16.9	17.3	7.5	8.3	8.6	41.9	29.3	28.5	17.1	16.3	17.2
Farming, forestry, and fishing	6.6	3.4	3.6	5.4	4.3	5.0	1.3	0.5	0.4	0.8	1.0	1.1
Precision production and crafts	15.5	15.6	15.9	21.6	21.3	20.4	2.4	2.3	2.6	2.7	2.3	2.2
Machine operators and assemblers	15.6	14.7	11.0	10.4	9.1	7.4	13.1	12.3	10.1	10.9	8.0	5.7
Transportation	11.6	11.1	9.7	7.2	6.9	6.5	0.5	0.9	1.2	0.5	0.8	0.9
Handlers, helpers, and laborers	15.4	11.5	13.5	6.4	5.7	5.7	3.2	2.9	2.0	2.4	2.0	1.3
Total	100.0	100.0	100.0	100.1	100.1	100.0	100.0	100.0	100.0	100.0	100.0	100.0

Source: Adapted from Reynolds Farley and Walter R. Allen, *The Color Line and the Quality of Life in America* (New York: Russell Sage Foundation, 1987), pp. 272–273, table 9.2. Data from U.S. Bureau of the Census: 1980, PC80-1-C1–A, table 89; PC80-1-D1–A, table 281; U.S. Bureau of Labor Statistics, *Employment and Earnings*, vol. 33, no. 5 (1986), table A–23.

[a]Employed persons aged 16 and over.

[b]April data.

Table 3–9

Percentage of Earned Degrees Conferred upon Women: 1950–1985

	Bachelor's[a]		Master's		Doctorate		Total	
	Total Number	Percent Women	Total Number	Percent Women	Total Number	Percent Women	Total Number	Percent Women
1950	434	23.9	58	29.3	6.6	9.1	499	24.4
1955	288	36.1	58	32.8	8.8	9.1	354	35.0
1960	395	35.1	75	32.0	9.8	10.2	479	34.2
1965	539	40.6	112	32.1	16.5	10.9	668	38.5
1970	833	41.5	209	39.7	29.9	13.4	1,073	40.4
1974	1,009	42.5	278	43.2	33.9	19.2	1,321	42.0
1975	988	43.5	294	44.9	34.1	21.4	1,316	43.2
1976	998	43.6	313	46.3	34.1	22.9	1,345	43.8
1977	993	44.4	318	46.9	33.3	24.3	1,344	44.6
1978	998	45.4	313	47.9	32.2	26.4	1,342	45.7
1979	1,000	46.6	302	50.0	32.8	28.0	1,335	46.7
1980[b]	999	47.3	298	49.3	32.6	29.8	1,330	47.4
1981[b]	1,007	48.0	296	50.3	32.9	31.0	1,336	48.2
1982[b]	1,025	48.6	296	50.7	32.7	32.1	1,353	48.8
1983[b]	1,042	49.1	290	50.0	32.8	33.2	1,365	48.9
1984[b]	1,049	49.0	285	49.5	33.3	33.6	1,366	48.8
1985[b]	1,055	49.4	286	50.0	32.9	34.0	1,374	49.3

Source: Adapted from U.S. Bureau of the Census, *Statistical Abstract of the U.S.* (Washington, D.C.: U.S. Government Printing Office, 1988), p. 149, table 254. Data from U.S. Department of Education, Center for Education Statistics, *Digest of Education Statistics*, annual.

Note: Numbers are in thousands. Except as noted, data include Puerto Rico. Beginning in 1960, data include Alaska and Hawaii.

[a]Includes first professional degrees.

[a]Data for fifty states and Washington, D.C.

They lagged the farthest behind men in engineering, where they represented less than 13 percent of the degrees conferred in 1986.

In the earlier edition, Simon (1975) reported that in 1969, "a much smaller proportion of the women in the professional and managerial categories, as opposed to the men, had completed at least four years of college" (p. 28). Sixty-one percent of the men in the professional categories had at least four years of college, compared to 12 percent of the women in the same occupational categories. Table 3–11 describes the 1987 scenario. Although the categories changed slightly (see the table footnote), instead of the 61 to 12 percent gap between men and women with more than four years of college in the highest-ranking occupational category, the difference in 1987 was only 8.5 percent, with 66 percent of the men and 57 percent of the women with postgraduate training.

Table 3–10

Percentage of Professional Degrees Conferred upon Women:
1960–1986

	Medicine (MD)		Denistry (DDS or DMD)		Law (LLB or JD)		Engineering	
	Total Number	Percent Women	Total Number	Percent Women	Total Number	Percent Women	Total Number	Percent Women
1960	7,032	5.5	3,247	0.8	9,240	2.5	45,624	0.4
1970	8,314	8.4	3,718	0.9	14,916	5.4	63,753	0.8
1975	12,447	13.1	4,773	3.1	29,296	15.1	65,308	2.2
1978	14,279	21.5	5,189	10.9	34,402	26.0	74,492	6.2
1979	14,786	23.0	5,434	11.8	35,206	28.5	80,376	7.7
1980	14,902	23.4	5,258	13.3	35,647	30.2	87,643	8.7
1981	15,505	24.7	5,460	14.4	36,331	32.4	94,270	9.7
1982	15,814	25.0	5,282	15.4	35,991	33.4	100,580	10.8
1983	15,484	26.7	5,585	17.1	36,853	36.4	111,451	11.6
1984	15,813	28.2	5,353	19.6	37,012	36.8	118,086	12.2
1985	16,041	30.4	5,339	20.7	37,491	38.5	120,892	12.5
1986	15,938	30.8	5,046	22.6	35,844	39.0	121,024	12.5

Source: 1960–1985: U.S. Bureau of the Census, *Statistical Abstract of the U.S.* (Washington, D.C.: U.S. Government Printing Office, 1988), p. 151, table 256; 1986: U.S. Bureau of the Census, *Statistical Abstract of the U.S.* (Washington, D.C.: U.S. Government Printing Office, 1989), p. 156, table 268. Data from U.S. Department of Education, Center for Education Statistics, *Digest of Education Statistics*, annual.

Overall, the occupational status and years of schooling for men and women showed much greater similarity in 1987 than in 1969. In 1987, the biggest difference between men and women occurred in categories 2 (technical, sales, and administration) and 3 (service), in which there were about one and a half times more college- and postcollege-trained men than women.

Income

Table 3–12 examines the factor that many people view as the most important indicator of women's equality: how much women earn compared to men. This table compares men's and women's incomes among blacks and whites. Looking first at the ratios of white men versus white women as opposed to black men versus black women, we see that the trends are in the opposite direction. Among blacks, male and female incomes moved closer together. In 1955, black females

Table 3–11
Educational Achievement for Males and Females over Twenty-five
Years of Age by Occupational Category: 1969 and 1987[a]

	1969											
	Males						Females					
	1	2	3	4	5	6	1	2	3	4	5	6
High school												
<4 years	5.9	22.4	29.4	23.6	51.8	62.1	37.4	26.9	20.0	38.7	52.0	68.7
4 years	16.2	32.1	41.9	35.0	38.0	31.7	39.5	42.5	59.5	46.9	38.1	28.5
College												
1–2 years	12.8	15.8	15.4	17.8	7.0	4.4	9.3	14.0	14.7	9.4	6.5	2.1
3 years	4.3	3.9	3.0	4.3	1.0	0.6	2.2	2.6	1.7	1.5	0.9	0.3
≥4 years	60.9	25.7	10.3	19.3	1.2	1.2	11.7	13.9	4.2	3.5	2.5	0.5
Total	100	100	100	100	99	100	100	100	100	100	100	100

	1987									
	Males						Females			
	1	2	3	4	5		1	2	3	4	5
High school										
<4 years	3.3	7.0	23.0	22.6	32.0		2.2	6.0	30.0	23.2	36.5
4 years	14.7	34.4	43.5	53.1	50.4		19.6	54.1	51.0	54.1	51.6
College										
1–3 years	16.3	28.0	22.8	18.3	13.4		21.0	26.3	14.0	13.8	8.6
≥4 years	65.7	30.5	10.7	6.0	4.2		57.2	13.6	5.0	8.9	3.3
Total	100	100	100	100	100		100	100	100	100	100

Source: Adapted from the 1970 U.S. Census of Population (U.S. Department of Commerce, 1973), Subject Reports; U.S. Bureau of Census, *Statistical Abstract of the U.S.* (Washington, D.C.: U.S. Government Printing Office, 1988), p. 379, table 629.

[a] Occupational categories in 1969: 1 = professional and technical; 2 = managerial and administration; 3 = clerical and kindred workers; 4 = sales; 5 = craftsmen and foremen; 6 = operatives. Occupational categories in 1987: 1 = managerial and professional; 2 = technical, sales, and administration; 3 = service; 4 = precision production; 5 = operators and fabricators.

earned slightly more than half of what black males earned. During the 1970s, black women began earning closer to 75 percent of what black men earned. Among whites, the earnings gap between men and women widened. In 1955, white women earned two-thirds of what white men earned. In the mid-sixties and up through 1980, they earned less than 60 percent of what white men earned. In 1982, white women's earnings were 62 percent of those of white men, the highest ratio since 1958.

Among women, the gap between blacks and whites narrowed considerably. In 1955, black women earned about half of what white women earned. In 1982,

Table 3–12
*Ratios of Median Annual Income of White and Black Women and
Men: 1955–1982*

	BF/WM	BF/BM	BF/WF	WF/WM	WF/BM	BM/WM
1955	0.34	0.55	0.51	0.65	1.07	0.61
1956	0.35	0.59	0.56	0.63	1.06	0.60
1957	0.37	0.61	0.58	0.64	1.04	0.61
1958	0.39	0.58	0.59	0.63	1.00	0.63
1959	0.41	0.67	0.64	0.61	1.05	0.58
1960	0.41	0.62	0.68	0.61	0.92	0.66
1961	0.39	0.61	0.66	0.59	0.93	0.63
1962	0.36	0.61	0.61	0.60	1.00	0.60
1963	0.37	0.57	0.62	0.59	0.92	0.64
1964	0.41	0.63	0.69	0.59	0.91	0.66
1965	0.39	0.63	0.68	0.58	0.92	0.63
1966	0.41	0.65	0.71	0.58	0.92	0.63
1967	0.43	0.65	0.75	0.57	0.86	0.67
1968	0.43	0.63	0.74	0.58	0.85	0.69
1969	0.47	0.70	0.82	0.58	0.85	0.68
1970	0.49	0.70	0.84	0.59	0.83	0.70
1971	0.52	0.74	0.90	0.58	0.82	0.71
1972	0.49	0.70	0.87	0.57	0.81	0.69
1973	0.49	0.69	0.87	0.56	0.80	0.70
1974	0.55	0.73	0.94	0.58	0.78	0.75
1975	0.57	0.75	0.98	0.58	0.76	0.77
1976	0.55	0.75	0.94	0.59	0.80	0.73
1977	0.55	0.77	0.95	0.58	0.80	0.72
1978	0.56	0.70	0.94	0.59	0.75	0.79
1979	0.55	0.73	0.93	0.59	0.78	0.75
1980	0.56	0.74	0.94	0.59	0.79	0.75
1981	0.55	0.74	0.92	0.60	0.80	0.74
1982	0.57	0.75	0.91	0.62	0.83	0.75

Source: Adapted from Bianchi and Spain 1986, p. 179, table 6.5. Data are from U.S. Bureau of the Census, "Money Income of Households, Families, and Persons in the United States: 1982," Current Population Reports, series P-60, no. 142 (Washington, D.C.: U.S. Government Printing Office, 1984), table 40.
Note: Data are for full-time, year-round workers; BF = black and other race females; WF = white females; BM = black and other race males; WM = white males.

the difference between black and white women's earnings was less than 10 percent.

Controlling for occupational categories does not reveal major gains by women between 1956 and 1986 (table 3–13). Professional, technical, managerial, and clerical women workers continued to earn about two-thirds of what men did in 1986. Among sales personnel and operators, the differential was greater. Women in those categories earned only 50 percent and 40 percent, respectively, of what men earned.

Table 3–13
Median Annual Income (in Dollars) by Type of Employment and by Sex and Ratio (R) of Female Earnings to Male Earnings: 1956–1986

	Professional and Technical			Managers and Officials			Clerical			Sales Workers			Operatives		
	Male	Female	R	Male	Female	R	Male	Female	R	Male	Female	R	Male	Female	R
1956	7,484	4,672	62	7,638	4,512	59	5,617	4,026	72	6,406	2,675	42	5,421	3,369	62
1957	7,410	4,713	64	7,558	4,812	64	5,646	4,066	72	6,362	2,831	45	5,439	3,230	59
1958	7,777	4,950	64	7,679	4,503	59	5,778	4,045	70	6,366	2,786	44	5,325	3,278	62
1959	8,161	5,236	64	8,251	4,697	57	6,125	4,171	68	6,621	2,794	42	5,501	3,482	63
1960	8,367	5,125	61	7,818	4,132	53	6,222	4,204	68	6,870	2,809	41	5,876	3,492	59
1961	8,685	5,670	65	8,114	3,967	49	6,228	4,325	69	7,002	2,781	40	5,989	3,432	57
1962	8,764	5,566	64	7,943	4,306	54	6,455	4,400	68	7,159	2,998	42	6,135	3,629	59
1963	9,073	5,658	62	8,337	4,282	51	6,662	4,469	67	7,426	2,758	37	6,297	3,539	56
1964	9,577	5,753	60	8,483	4,170	49	6,930	4,540	66	7,755	3,052	39	6,394	3,640	57
1965	9,330	6,082	65	8,708	4,635	53	6,927	4,658	67	7,970	3,232	41	6,378	3,610	57
1966	9,868	6,195	63	9,461	4,794	51	7,013	4,626	66	8,097	3,287	41	6,577	3,631	55
1967	10,193	6,590	65	9,691	5,182	54	7,037	4,688	67	8,080	3,380	42	6,576	3,783	58
1968	10,542	6,610	63	9,794	5,101	52	7,324	4,778	65	8,292	3,388	41	6,773	3,956	58
1969	11,151	6,935	62	10,453	5,549	53	7,537	4,898	65	8,762	3,519	40	6,950	4,082	59
1979	21,310	13,701	64	21,835	11,705	54	16,503	9,855	60	17,084	8,880	52	14,921	8,562	57
1980	23,026	15,285	66	23,558	12,936	55	18,247	10,997	60	19,910	9,748	49	15,702	9,440	60
1981	25,653	16,508	64	25,425	14,820	58	18,938	11,755	62	22,331	11,238	50	16,948	10,301	40

	Executive Administrative, and Managerial			Professional Specialty			Technical and Related Support			Administrative Support			Sales			Operatives		
	Male	Female	R	Male	Female	R	Male	Female	R	Male	Female	R	Male	Female	R	Male	Female	R
1985	33,530	20,565	61	32,814	21,781	66	26,266	18,177	69	22,997	15,157	66	25,445	12,682	50	20,786	12,232	59
1986	34,962	21,432	61	35,143	23,076	66	27,880	19,236	69	22,718	15,509	68	26,803	12,956	48	20,551	12,324	60

Source: 1956–1969: Adapted from Abbot L. Feris, *Indicators of Trends in the Status of American Women* (New York: Russell Sage Foundation, 1971); 1979–1981 and 1985–1986: U.S. Bureau of the Census, *Statistical Abstract of the U.S.* (Washington, D.C.: U.S. Government Printing Office, 1980, table 679; 1981, table 670; 1982, table 715; 1986, table 681; 1987, table 653.

Conclusion

The picture of the current status of the American woman that emerges from these statistics is that changes have occurred in some areas but not in others. More women are delaying marriage, more are getting divorced, more are heads of households, and more are in the labor force full-time. The positions that women occupy in the labor force demonstrate upward mobility from clerical and sales positions to managerial, professional, and technical positions. But there has been little change in the income ratios of men and women for the same job classifications.

The primary objectives and goals of the contemporary women's movement are to move women into jobs that carry more prestige, authority, and monetary compensation. Thus, success should be measured by the proportion of women in managerial and professional positions, the proportion of women who have completed college and obtained professional degrees, and the absence of lower salary scales for women in the same types of jobs as men. On the first two measures, the status of women has improved. On the last measure, there is little evidence of improvement.

4

Arrest Statistics

With this chapter, we begin our examination of crime data looking first at the statistics concerning the proportion of women as opposed to men who have been arrested for different types of crimes over the past 25 years.

Longitudinal, national data about the number of women involved in crimes and the types of crimes with which they are charged have been available since 1930, when the Federal Bureau of Investigation (FBI) published its first *Uniform Crime Report (UCR)*. This annual report, currently based on data obtained from approximately ten thousand law enforcement agencies across the country, describes the number of arrests in a given year, the offenses for which suspects were arrested, and the age, sex, and racial backgrounds of those arrested. Arrest rates and trends are shown by cities, suburbs, and rural areas, as well as for the United States as a whole.

The FBI divides specific crimes for which arrest data are available into two categories. Type I offenses include the following:

- Criminal homicide, including murder and nonnegligent manslaughter and manslaughter by negligence

- Forcible rape

- Robbery

- Aggravated assault

- Burglary

- Larceny

- Auto theft

- Arson (as of 1979)

Type I offenses are used to establish an Index in the Uniform Crime Reporting Program (hereafter referred to as the Crime Index) to measure the trend and distribution of crime in the United States. These particular offenses were selected because "they represent the most common local crime problem. They are all serious crimes either by their nature or due to the volume in which they occur" (F.B.I., 1987).

Type II offenses include the following:

- Other assaults

- Forgery and counterfeiting

- Fraud

- Embezzlement

- Stolen property (buying, receiving, or possessing)

- Vandalism

- Weapons (carrying, possessing, and so on)

- Prostitution and commercialized vice

- Sex offenses (except forcible rape, prostitution, and commercialized vice)

- Narcotic drug law violations

- Gambling

- Offenses against the family and children

- Driving under the influence

- Liquor law violations

- Drunkenness

- Disorderly conduct

- Vagrancy

- All other offenses.

This chapter deals primarily with Type I offenses, as they are the most serious and common. Rape is not included because it is almost exclusively a male offense.[1] We do comment on some Type II offenses, usually because there has been a change in the arrest pattern for women or the arrest rates for women have been consistently high.

As this chapter unfolds, it may appear that we are using arrest statistics as proxies for crime rates without regard for the hazards of doing so. We are aware of the dangers of using the terms *arrest* and *crimes committed* interchangeably and know that arrest statistics may not be the most reliable source of data for determining actual crime rates. Unfortunately, no other data provide information about the characteristics of the suspect as well as the offense.[2] Another problem with the data is that the number of agencies reporting to the *UCR* varies from year to year, sometimes drastically. Between 1963 and 1967, the number of reporting agencies ranged from a low of 3,977 in 1964 to a high of 12,811 in 1981. These differences, however, are only of concern when considering the raw numbers reported. They need not affect the validity of proportional trends within and between gender groupings.

Criminologists usually prefer to use statistics computed on the basis of crimes known to the police for determining crime rates, but unfortunately those statistics do not identify the suspect in any way. We use arrest data to describe female crime patterns and to compare male and female arrests for different types of offenses because they are the only data that distinguish between men and women and that are available on a long-term basis. We also recognize that the proportions of arrests vary considerably from one type of offense to another. For example, the proportion of all Type I crimes that were cleared by arrest in 1987 was 20.9 percent, but violent crimes were much more likely to be cleared by arrest than property crimes—47.4 percent versus 17.7 percent. A further breakdown of the Type I offenses that were cleared by arrest reveal the following pattern: murder, 70 percent; forcible rape, 52.9 percent; aggravated assault, 59 percent; robbery, 26.5 percent; burglary, 13.8 percent; larceny, 19.8 percent; auto theft, 45.3 percent; and arson, 15.8 percent. Arrest rates are obviously more accurate proxies for behavior in violent crimes than they are for behavior in property crimes, and the more serious the crime, the more accurate the proxy.

With these qualifications and precautions in mind, we turn to the arrest data and report first the proportion of women who were arrested for all types of crimes as well as for those crimes included in the Crime Index from 1963 to 1987 (table 4–1). This table also describes the overall rate of change in the proportion of women arrested in both categories for the following time periods: 1963–1987, 1973–1987, and 1980–1987.

Table 4–1 shows that in 1987, 1 out of every 5.7 persons arrested was a woman. The rate of change over the twenty-five-year period was .55. In 1963, 1 out of 8.6 persons arrested for a serious crime was a woman. In 1987, the proportion had dropped to 1 out of 4.6. The overall rate of increase was .85 for the entire period. The overall increase in the proportion of women arrested for serious crimes was greater than the overall increase in the proportion of women arrested for all crimes. Note also that over the entire period, the percentage of women arrested for serious crimes was greater than the percentage of women arrested for all offenses.

Table 4–2 reports the proportions of female and male arrests for serious crimes as a percentage of total male and female arrests for all crimes. In 1963, 1 out of 6.3 women arrested were arrested for a serious crime, as opposed to

Table 4–1
Females Arrested for All Crimes and for Serious Crimes: 1963–1987

	Total Arrested for All Crimes	Percent Female	Total Arrested for Serious Crimes	Percent Female
1963	4,510,835	11.4	695,222	11.7
1964	4,685,080	11.7	780,501	12.6
1965	5,031,393	11.9	834,296	13.4
1966	5,016,407	12.2	871,962	13.9
1967	5,518,420	12.5	996,800	14.1
1968	5,616,839	12.9	1,047,220	14.2
1969	5,862,246	13.7	1,111,674	15.7
1970	6,570,473	14.4	1,273,783	16.9
1971	6,966,822	15.0	1,397,304	17.2
1972	7,013,194	15.1	1,417,115	18.0
1973	6,499,864	15.3	1,372,220	18.7
1974	6,179,406	16.1	1,474,427	19.0
1975	8,013,645	15.7	1,901,811	19.5
1976	7,912,348	15.7	1,787,106	19.8
1977	9,029,335	16.0	1,986,043	20.1
1978	9,775,087	15.8	2,169,262	19.9
1979	9,506,347	15.7	2,163,302	19.5
1980	9,703,181	15.8	2,198,077	18.8
1981	10,293,575	16.1	2,293,754	19.1
1982	10,062,343	16.3	2,152,480	19.7
1983	10,287,309	16.6	2,151,120	20.1
1984	8,921,708	16.7	1,834,348	20.8
1985	10,289,609	17.4	2,124,671	21.4
1986	10,392,177	17.4	2,167,071	21.1
1987	10,795,869	17.7	2,266,467	21.6
Overall rate of change				
1963–87		0.55		0.85
1973–87		0.16		0.16
1980–87		0.12		0.15

Source: Adapted from *Uniform Crime Report* (Washington, D.C.: U.S. Department of Justice, Federal Bureau of Investigation, annual; 1963–1987). Total Arrests, Distribution by Sex.

slightly less than 1 out of 6.5 men arrested. Two and a half decades later, a higher proportion of women than men were arrested for serious offenses (1 out of 3.9 for women versus 1 out of 5 for men). Note that the percentage of females and males arrested for serious offenses peaked in the late 1970s, then declined slightly such that the 1987 figures are about the same as those reported in 1973.

Table 4–3 describes the proportion of women arrested for all serious (Type I) crimes and for all Type I violent and property offenses. This table disputes a popular myth that women have been committing crimes of violence at a much

Table 4–2
Males and Females Arrested for Serious Crimes as a Percentage of Their Respective Sex Cohorts
Arrested for All Crimes: 1963–1987

	Total Females Arrested (All Crimes)	Females Arrested for Serious Crimes as Percent of All Females Arrested	Total Males Arrested (All Crimes)	Males Arrested for Serious Crimes as Percent of All Males Arrested	Difference between Females and Males Arrested for Serious Crimes (Percent)
1963	513,851	15.8	3,996,984	15.3	0.5
1964	546,981	18.0	4,138,099	16.5	1.5
1965	599,768	18.7	4,431,625	16.3	2.4
1966	609,768	19.8	4,406,639	17.0	2.8
1967	688,502	20.4	4,829,918	17.7	2.7
1968	725,496	20.5	4,891,343	18.4	2.1
1969	804,046	21.7	5,058,200	18.5	3.2
1970	946,897	22.8	5,623,576	18.8	4.0
1971	1,043,770	23.1	5,923,052	19.5	3.6
1972	1,057,411	24.1	5,955,783	19.5	4.6
1973	997,580	25.8	5,502,284	20.3	5.5
1974	994,296	28.2	5,185,110	23.0	5.2
1975	1,262,100	29.4	6,751,545	22.7	6.7
1976	1,240,439	28.6	6,671,909	21.5	7.1
1977	1,448,073	27.5	7,581,262	20.9	6.6
1978	1,547,859	27.9	8,227,228	21.1	6.8
1979	1,494,930	28.2	8,011,417	21.7	6.5
1980	1,532,934	27.0	8,170,247	21.8	5.2
1981	1,660,167	26.4	8,633,408	21.5	4.9
1982	1,637,180	25.9	8,425,163	20.5	5.4
1983	1,705,486	25.4	8,581,823	20.0	5.4
1984	1,489,100	25.6	7,432,608	19.6	6.0
1985	1,790,504	25.3	8,499,105	19.7	5.6
1986	1,805,849	25.3	8,586,328	19.9	5.4
1987	1,914,341	25.6	8,881,528	20.0	5.6
Overall rate of change					
1963–87	0.62			0.30	
1973–87	−0.01			−0.01	
1980–87	−0.05			−0.08	

Source: Adapted from *Uniform Crime Report* (Washington, D.C.: U.S. Department of Justice, Federal Bureau of Investigation, annual; 1963–1987). Total Arrests, Distribution by Sex.

Table 4–3

Percentage of Females Arrested for All Serious (Type I) Crimes and for All Type I Violent and Property Crimes: 1963–1987

	Total Arrested for Serious Crimes	Percent Female	Total Arrested for Violent Crimes[a]	Percent Female	Total Arrested for Property Crimes[b]	Percent Female
1963	695,222	11.7	124,821	10.3	570,401	12.0
1964	780,501	12.6	137,576	10.4	642,925	13.0
1965	834,296	13.4	151,180	10.2	683,116	14.1
1966	871,962	13.9	167,780	10.1	704,182	14.8
1967	996,800	14.1	191,807	9.8	804993.0	15.1
1968	1,047,220	14.2	201,813	9.5	845,407	15.4
1969	1,111,674	15.7	216,194	9.6	892,283	17.1
1970	1,273,783	16.9	241,905	9.6	1,028,858	18.7
1971	1,397,304	17.2	273,209	10.0	1,121,327	19.0
1972	1,417,115	18.0	299,221	10.0	1,114,908	20.2
1973	1,372,220	18.7	290,382	10.2	1,078,842	21.1
1974	1,474,427	19.0	294,617	10.2	1,177,584	21.2
1975	1,901,811	19.5	370,453	10.3	1,528,317	21.7
1976	1,787,106	19.8	338,849	10.5	1,445,607	22.1
1977	1,986,043	20.1	386,806	10.4	1,596,304	22.4
1978	2,169,262	19.9	446,122	10.2	1,723,140	22.4
1979	2,163,302	19.5	434,778	10.2	1,728,524	21.8
1980	2,198,077	18.8	446,373	10.0	1,751,704	21.0
1981	2,293,754	19.1	464,826	10.1	1,828,928	21.4
1982	2,152,480	19.7	443,860	10.4	1,708,620	22.1
1983	2,151,120	20.1	443,686	10.8	1,707,434	22.5
1984	1,834,348	20.8	382,246	10.7	1,452,102	23.4
1985	2,124,671	21.4	431,332	10.9	1,693,339	24.0
1986	2,167,071	21.1	465,391	10.9	1,701,680	23.9
1987	2,266,467	21.6	473,030	11.1	1,793,437	24.4
Overall rate of change						
1963–87		0.85		0.08		1.03
1973–87		0.16		0.09		0.16
1980–87		0.15		0.11		0.16

Source: Adapted from *Uniform Crime Report* (Washington, D.C.: U.S. Department of Justice, Federal Bureau of Investigation, annual; 1963–1987). Total Arrests, Distribution by Sex.

[a]Includes males and females arrested for criminal homicide, forcible rape, robbery, and aggravated assault.
[b]Includes males and females arrested for burglary, larceny/theft, and auto theft. Beginning in 1979, arson also is included.

higher rate in recent years than in the more distant past. In fact, the increase in the proportion of female arrests for serious crimes may be explained almost fully by the fact that women seem to be committing more *property* offenses than they did in the past. Indeed, the percentage of women arrested for crimes of violence does not show a marked change. Between 1963 and 1987, the percentage fluctuated only slightly, from a low of 9.5 percent in 1968 to a high of 11.1 percent in 1987. But the picture for property offenses is markedly different. In 1963, 1 out of 8.3 arrests was a woman. In 1987, 1 out of 4.1 persons arrested for a serious property crime was a woman. Again, the greatest escalation in female property offenses occurred prior to 1973. From 1973 on, the gender proportions of property offenders remained relatively stable.

Table 4–4 demonstrates the same phenomenon in the comparison of men and women who were arrested for violent and property offenses versus those arrested for all serious offenses between 1963 and 1987. The proportion of men who were arrested for violent offenses increased by .30 over the twenty-five-year period, while the proportion of women *decreased* by .32. For both males and females, the bulk of the changes occurred between 1963 and 1973. For property offenses, the trend is negligible and in the opposite direction. The proportion of serious female offenders who were arrested for crimes against property increased by .06, while the proportion of serious male offenders arrested for property crimes decreased by .07.

Table 4–5 provides more details about the types of serious property and violent offenses for which women were arrested. Note that women accounted for almost one-third of all arrests for larceny in 1987. Also note that this proportion did not change much from the proportion in the early 1970s. The big increase in women's arrests for larceny occurred between 1963 and 1973. Female arrests for criminal homicide and aggravated assault remained stable over the full twenty-five-year period, ranging from 15.5 to 12.5 percent and from 14.0 to 12.4 percent, respectively. While burglary and auto theft were still dominated by men in 1987, women's participation showed a marked increase. Burglary, perhaps more than any other offense examined thus far, requires skills that are usually acquired within a criminal subculture. Because women have not been part of such criminal networks, their opportunities for acquiring these skills have been much more limited. Even with increased female participation in burglary and auto theft, women did not account for more than 10 percent of the arrests in either of those crime categories.

Table 4–6 compares the proportions of men and women arrested for the same Type I offenses shown in table 4–5 as a percentage of the total arrests for all crimes. These data show that within all the violent crime categories, the differences in arrest rates between men and women were either nonexistent or slight. For criminal homicide, the percentage of males and females remained remarkably stable between 1963 and 1987. For robbery and aggravated assault, males maintained a small but steady edge over females.

The most striking change was in arrests for larceny. From 1963 to 1987, the rate of increase for women was 25 percent greater than the rate of increase for men. In 1963, about 1 out of every 8.6 women arrested was arrested for larceny. In 1987, the ratio was down to just less than 1 out of 5. For males, the proportion shifted from 1 out of 15.6 in 1963 to 1 out of 10.3 in 1987.

Table 4–4
Females and Males Arrested for Violent and Property Crimes as a Percentage of All Arrests for Serious Crimes in Their Respective Sex Cohorts: 1963–1987

	Total Females Arrested for Serious Crimes	Percent of Females Arrested for Violent Crimes	Percent of Females Arrested for Property Crimes	Total Males Arrested for Serious Crimes	Percent of Males Arrested for Violent Crimes	Percent of Males Arrested for Property Crimes
1963	81,357	15.8	84.2	613,865	18.2	81.8
1964	98,186	14.6	85.4	682,315	18.1	81.9
1965	111,972	13.7	86.3	722,324	18.8	81.2
1966	120,872	14.0	86.0	751,090	20.1	79.9
1967	140,405	13.4	86.6	856,395	20.2	79.8
1968	149,060	12.8	87.2	898,160	20.3	79.7
1969	174,079	12.0	87.8	937,595	20.8	78.9
1970	215,614	10.8	89.1	1,058,169	20.7	79.1
1971	240,979	11.4	88.5	1,156,325	21.3	78.5
1972	255,205	11.7	88.1	1,161,910	23.2	76.6
1973	257,081	11.5	88.4	1,115,139	23.4	76.4
1974	279,811	10.8	89.1	1,194,616	22.1	77.7
1975	370,711	10.3	89.6	1,531,100	21.7	78.1
1976	354,732	10.0	89.9	1,432,374	21.2	78.6
1977	398,625	10.1	89.8	1,587,418	21.8	78.0
1978	431,809	10.5	89.5	1,737,453	23.1	76.9
1979	421,320	10.5	89.5	1,741,982	22.4	77.6
1980	413,138	10.8	89.2	1,784,939	22.5	77.5
1981	438,913	10.7	89.3	1,854,841	22.5	77.5
1982	423,602	10.9	89.1	1,728,878	23.0	77.0
1983	432,809	11.1	88.9	1,718,311	23.0	77.0
1984	380,633	10.7	89.3	1,453,715	23.5	76.5
1985	453,799	10.3	89.7	1,670,872	23.0	77.0
1986	457,152	11.1	88.9	1,709,919	24.2	75.8
1987	489,809	10.7	89.3	1,776,658	23.7	76.3
Overall rate of change						
1963–87		−0.32	0.06		0.30	−0.07
1973–87		−0.07	0.01		0.01	0.00
1980–87		−0.01	0.00		0.05	−0.02

Source: Adapted from *Uniform Crime Report* (Washington, D.C.: U.S. Department of Justice, Federal Bureau of Investigation, annual; 1963–1987) Total Arrests, Distribution by Sex.

Table 4-5
Females Arrested as a Percentage of All Arrests for Type I Offenses: 1963–1987

Year	Total Arrested for Criminal Homicide	Percent Female	Total Arrested for Robbery	Percent Female	Total Arrested for Aggravated Assault	Percent Female	Total Arrested for Burglary	Percent Female	Total Arrested for Larceny	Percent Female	Total Arrested for Auto Theft	Percent Female
1963	8,805	15.5	37,836	4.9	68,719	14.0	170,160	3.3	314,402	19.0	85,839	3.7
1964	9,097	15.5	39,134	5.3	79,895	13.6	187,000	3.7	358,569	20.3	97,356	4.2
1965	10,163	15.4	45,872	5.2	84,411	13.5	197,627	3.7	383,726	22.1	101,763	4.2
1966	10,734	15.3	47,031	5.0	98,406	13.2	199,781	3.9	398,623	23.1	105,778	4.1
1967	12,167	14.8	59,789	5.2	107,192	12.9	239,461	4.1	447,299	23.9	118,233	4.2
1968	13,538	14.7	69,115	5.6	106,475	12.4	256,216	4.2	463,928	24.4	125,263	4.9
1969	14,706	14.1	76,533	6.2	113,724	12.6	255,937	4.4	510,660	26.5	125,686	5.3
1970	15,856	14.5	87,687	6.1	125,971	12.6	285,418	4.7	616,099	27.9	127,341	5.1
1971	17,317	15.7	101,728	6.3	140,350	13.3	315,376	4.9	674,997	28.1	130,954	6.0
1972	18,035	14.8	109,217	6.5	155,581	13.2	314,393	5.2	678,673	29.7	121,842	5.7
1973	17,395	14.5	101,894	6.8	154,891	13.2	316,272	5.4	644,190	31.5	107,226	6.5
1974	16,044	14.3	108,481	6.8	154,514	13.4	340,697	5.4	729,661	30.7	120,224	7.0
1975	19,526	14.9	129,217	7.0	202,217	13.1	449,155	5.4	958,938	31.2	110,708	7.0
1976	16,763	14.1	110,296	7.1	192,753	13.1	406,821	5.2	928,078	31.2	135,196	7.0
1977	20,096	14.0	122,514	7.4	221,329	12.8	454,193	6.0	1,006,915	31.8	153,270	8.3
1978	18,755	14.1	141,481	7.0	257,629	12.7	485,782	6.1	1,084,088	31.7	153,270	8.3
1979	18,264	13.7	130,753	7.4	256,597	12.4	468,085	6.3	1,098,398	30.3	143,654	8.9
1980	18,745	12.8	139,476	7.2	258,721	12.4	479,639	6.2	1,123,823	28.9	129,783	8.6
1981	20,432	12.7	147,396	7.2	266,948	12.6	489,533	6.3	1,197,845	29.1	122,188	8.9
1982	18,511	13.3	138,118	7.3	258,899	12.9	436,271	6.6	1,146,705	29.4	108,736	9.0
1983	18,064	13.3	134,018	7.4	261,421	13.5	415,651	6.8	1,169,066	29.5	105,514	8.9
1984	13,676	13.3	108,614	7.2	231,620	13.4	334,399	7.4	1,009,743	30.2	93,285	9.2
1985	15,777	12.4	120,501	7.6	263,120	13.5	381,875	7.4	1,179,066	31.0	115,621	9.3
1986	16,066	12.3	124,245	7.8	293,952	13.2	375,544	7.9	1,182,099	30.7	128,514	9.5
1987	16,714	12.5	123,306	8.1	301,734	13.3	374,963	7.9	1,256,552	31.1	146,753	9.7
Overall rate of change												
1963–87		−0.19		0.66		−0.05		1.42		0.64		1.60
1973–87		−0.14		0.19		0.01		0.46		−0.01		0.49
1980–87		−0.02		0.12		0.07		0.27		0.08		0.13

Source: Adapted from *Uniform Crime Report* (Washington, D.C.: U.S. Department of Justice, Federal Bureau of Investigation, annual; 1963–1987). Total Arrests, Distribution by Sex.

Table 4-6
Females and Males Arrested for Serious Crimes as a Percentage of Their Total Arrests in Their Respective Sex Cohorts: 1963–1987

	Criminal Homicide		Robbery		Aggravated Assault		Burglary		Larceny/ Theft		Auto Theft	
	Female	Male	Female	Male	Female	Male	Female	Male	Female	Male	Female	Male
1963	0.3	0.2	0.4	0.9	1.9	1.5	1.1	4.1	11.6	6.4	0.6	2.1
1964	0.2	0.2	0.4	0.9	2.0	1.7	1.3	4.4	13.3	6.9	0.8	2.3
1965	0.2	0.2	0.4	1.0	1.9	1.6	1.2	4.3	14.2	6.7	0.7	2.2
1966	0.3	0.2	0.4	1.0	2.1	1.9	1.3	4.4	15.1	7.0	0.7	2.3
1967	0.2	0.3	0.5	1.2	2.0	1.9	1.4	4.8	15.5	7.0	0.7	2.3
1968	0.2	0.3	0.5	1.3	1.8	1.9	1.5	5.0	15.6	7.2	0.9	2.4
1969	0.2	0.3	0.6	1.4	1.8	2.0	1.4	4.8	16.8	7.4	0.8	2.4
1970	0.2	0.2	0.6	1.5	1.7	2.0	1.4	4.8	18.2	7.9	0.7	2.1
1971	0.2	0.2	0.6	1.6	1.8	2.1	1.5	5.1	18.2	8.2	0.7	2.1
1972	0.2	0.2	0.7	1.7	1.9	2.3	1.5	5.0	19.1	8.0	0.7	1.9
1973	0.2	0.2	0.7	1.7	2.1	2.4	1.7	5.4	20.4	8.0	0.7	2.0
1974	0.2	0.2	0.7	1.9	2.1	2.6	1.9	6.2	22.5	9.8	0.7	1.9
1975	0.2	0.2	0.7	1.8	2.1	2.6	1.9	6.3	23.7	9.8	0.7	1.7
1976	0.2	0.2	0.6	1.5	2.0	2.5	1.7	5.8	23.4	9.6	0.6	1.5
1977	0.2	0.2	0.6	1.5	2.0	2.5	1.9	5.6	22.1	9.1	0.8	1.6
1978	0.2	0.2	0.6	1.6	2.1	2.7	1.9	5.5	22.2	9.0	0.8	1.7
1979	0.2	0.2	0.6	1.5	2.1	2.8	2.0	5.5	22.2	9.6	0.9	1.6
1980	0.2	0.2	0.7	1.6	2.0	2.8	1.9	5.5	21.2	9.8	0.7	1.5
1981	0.2	0.2	0.6	1.6	2.0	2.7	1.8	5.3	21.0	9.8	0.7	1.3
1982	0.2	0.2	0.2	1.5	2.0	2.7	1.8	4.8	20.6	9.6	0.6	1.2
1983	0.1	0.2	0.6	1.4	2.1	2.6	1.7	4.5	20.2	9.6	0.6	1.1
1984	0.1	0.2	0.5	1.4	2.1	2.7	1.7	4.2	20.5	9.5	0.6	1.1
1985	0.1	0.2	0.5	1.3	2.0	2.7	1.6	4.2	20.4	9.6	0.6	1.2
1986	0.1	0.2	0.5	1.3	2.1	3.0	1.6	4.0	20.1	9.5	0.7	1.4
1987	0.1	0.2	0.5	1.3	2.1	2.9	1.6	3.9	20.4	9.7	0.7	1.5
Overall rate of change												
1963–87	−0.67	0.00	0.25	0.44	0.11	0.93	0.45	−0.05	0.76	0.52	0.17	−0.29
1973–87	−0.50	0.00	−0.29	−0.24	0.00	0.21	−0.06	−0.28	0.00	0.21	0.00	−0.25
1980–87	−0.50	0.00	−0.29	−0.19	0.00	0.04	−0.16	−0.29	−0.04	−0.01	0.00	0.00

Source: Adapted from *Uniform Crime Report* (Washington, D.C.: U.S. Department of Justice, Federal Bureau of Investigation, annual; 1963–1987). Total Arrests, Distribution by Sex.

Comparing the data in tables 4–5 and 4–6, we note that women's share of all larceny arrests remained stable from the early 1970s to 1987, but among all women arrested, larceny accounted for at least 20 percent of the arrests. Larceny, as we show later, accounts for more female arrests than any other offense in both the Type I and Type II categories.

Tables 4–7 and 4–8 describe trends in the proportion of female arrests for selective offenses in the Type II category. Table 4–7 shows that offenses against the family increased the most during the 1980s, although women and men still differed greatly in their rate of offending. Perhaps arrest rates for this crime more than for any other have been affected by changes in reporting behaviors and police response. However, if we look at table 4–8, we see that arrests for offenses against the family made up a negligible proportion of all females and males arrested.

The figures in Table 4–7 also show that in 1987, less than 1 out of 3 persons arrested for embezzlement and for forgery and counterfeiting was a woman, and almost 1 out of 2.5 arrests for fraud involved a woman. Unlike larceny, the proportion of female arrests for these property offenses was on the increase. If this trend persists, approximately equal percentages of men and women are likely to be arrested for fraud by the year 2000 and for embezzlement, forgery, and counterfeiting by the 2010s. Again, however, if we look at table 4–8, we see that only a negligible proportion of females and males were arrested for embezzlement and forgery/counterfeiting.

Fraud is a different story. Beginning in the late 1970s, it accounted for a fair proportion of female arrests, a proportion that exceeded arrests for prostitution and was slightly greater than those for drug law violations. But unlike drug law violations, it accounted for relatively little of the crime for which males were arrested.

Table 4–9 ranks the proportion of men and women who were arrested in 1972, 1980, and 1987 for the ten most frequently cited Type I and Type II offenses. These ten offenses accounted for 64.4 percent of all men and 66.4 percent of all women arrested in 1987.

Among the women, larceny remained the number one offense for which women were arrested. In 1987, women were less likely than in earlier years to be arrested for drunkenness and disorderly conduct but more likely to be arrested for drunken driving. Also, in 1980 and 1987, women were much more likely to be arrested for fraud than they were in 1972. For all the other offenses, the pattern remained fairly stable from 1972 to 1987. Given all the media coverage of drugs and crime, it is somewhat surprising that drugs accounted for only 6.3 percent of all female arrests in 1987. In contrast, crimes that specifically involved alcohol accounted for a total of 16.2 percent of all female offenses in 1987, which was similar to the percentages in the other two years (16.2 percent in 1972 and 17.4 percent in 1980).

Table 4-7
Females Arrested for Some Type II Crimes as a Percentage of All People Arrested for Various Crimes: 1963–1987

	Total Arrests for Embezzlement	Percent Female	Total Arrests for Fraud	Percent Female	Total Arrests for Forgery/Counterfeiting	Percent Female	Total Arrests for Offenses against the Family	Percent Female	Total Arrests for Narcotic Drug Law Violations	Percent Female	Total Arrests for Prostitution and Vice	Percent Female
1963[a]					30,610	17.6	58,228	9.1	29,604	14.2	26,124	76.9
1964	8,610	17.3	45,998	19.0	30,637	18.2	57,454	9.3	37,802	14.0	28,190	78.0
1965	7,674	17.2	52,007	20.3	30,617	18.4	60,981	8.8	46,069	13.4	33,987	77.5
1966	6,439	19.2	52,041	21.6	29,277	19.8	55,820	9.9	60,358	13.8	34,376	79.5
1967	6,073	19.2	58,192	23.2	33,462	20.8	56,137	8.9	101,079	13.7	39,744	77.7
1968	5,894	19.6	56,710	24.0	34,497	21.8	51,319	8.8	162,177	15.0	42,338	78.3
1969	6,309	20.8	63,445	26.2	36,727	22.7	50,312	9.2	232,690	15.5	46,410	79.6
1970	8,174	24.6	76,861	27.1	43,833	23.7	56,620	8.9	346,412	15.7	49,344	79.3
1971	7,114	24.9	95,610	28.6	45,340	24.5	56,456	8.6	400,606	16.3	52,916	77.7
1972	6,744	26.3	96,713	29.6	44,313	24.8	52,935	9.3	431,608	15.7	44,744	74.1
1973	5,612	23.7	85,467	31.2	41,975	26.7	42,784	9.2	484,242	14.5	45,308	75.5
1974	5,891	26.3	91,176	32.6	39,741	28.6	34,902	11.9	454,948	14.2	53,309	75.6
1975	9,302	31.1	146,253	34.2	57,803	28.9	53,332	11.7	508,189	13.8	50,229	74.3
1976	8,218	31.0	161,429	36.6	55,791	29.6	58,249	10.7	500,540	13.6	58,648	70.7
1977	6,607	22.7	216,672	35.6	67,984	29.1	53,385	10.3	569,293	13.9	77,115	70.7
1978	7,670	25.1	249,207	36.8	73,269	29.7	54,014	10.2	596,940	13.7	89,365	67.7
1979	7,882	25.3	243,461	40.4	70,977	30.9	53,321	9.9	519,377	13.5	83,088	67.5
1980	7,885	28.5	261,787	41.4	72,643	31.1	49,991	10.6	533,010	13.4	85,815	69.5
1981	8,170	28.5	272,900	41.2	81,429	32.1	51,908	10.5	586,646	13.2	103,134	73.4
1982	7,358	30.3	265,663	40.3	79,951	32.6	45,432	11.6	565,182	13.6	111,029	71.0
1983	7,604	32.4	261,844	40.2	74,508	33.4	46,111	11.1	616,936	14.0	119,262	70.2
1984	6,290	36.9	203,175	40.4	63,359	33.7	32,877	13.9	562,255	13.9	88,337	69.9
1985	9,799	35.6	286,941	42.6	75,281	33.2	48,699	12.7	702,882	13.8	101,167	69.5
1986	10,500	36.4	284,790	43.3	76,546	33.9	47,327	15.0	691,882	14.5	96,882	65.4
1987	10,639	38.1	280,809	43.5	78,817	34.4	48,002	17.4	811,078	14.9	100,950	64.8
Overall rate of change												
1963–87[b]	1.21		1.28		0.96		0.90		0.05		−0.16	
1973–87	0.61		0.39		0.29		0.89		0.03		−0.14	
1980–87	0.34		0.05		0.11		0.64		0.11		−0.07	

Source: Adapted from *Uniform Crime Report* (Washington, D.C.: U.S. Department of Justice, Federal Bureau of Investigation, annual; 1963–1987). Total Arrests, Distribution by Sex.

[a]In 1963, embezzlement and fraud were combined.

[b]For embezzlement and fraud, the rates are for the change from 1964 to 1987.

Table 4-6

Females and Males Arrested for Various Type II Crimes as a Percentage of All Arrests in Their Respective Sex Cohorts: 1963–1987

	Embezzlement		Fraud		Forgery and Counterfeiting		Offenses against the Family and Children		Narcotic Drug Law Violations		Prostitution and Vice	
	Female	Male	Female	Male	Female	Male	Female	Male	Female	Male	Female	Male
1963[a]	0.3	0.2	1.6	0.9	1.0	0.6	1.3	1.0	0.8	0.6	3.9	0.2
1964	0.2	0.1	1.8	0.9	1.0	0.6	1.0	1.3	1.0	0.8	4.0	1.0
1965	0.2	0.1	1.8	0.9	0.9	0.6	0.9	1.3	1.0	0.9	4.4	0.2
1966	0.2	0.1	2.0	0.9	0.9	0.5	0.9	1.1	1.4	1.2	4.5	0.2
1967	0.2	0.1	1.9	0.9	1.0	0.5	0.7	1.1	2.0	1.8	4.5	0.2
1968	0.2	0.1	2.1	0.9	1.0	0.6	0.6	1.0	3.3	2.8	4.6	0.2
1969	0.2	0.1	2.1	0.9	1.0	0.6	0.6	0.9	4.5	3.9	4.6	0.2
1970	0.2	0.1	2.2	1.0	1.1	0.6	0.5	0.9	5.7	5.2	4.1	0.2
1971	0.2	0.1	2.6	1.2	1.1	0.6	0.5	0.9	6.1	5.7	3.9	0.2
1972	0.2	0.1	2.7	1.1	1.0	0.6	0.5	0.8	6.3	6.1	3.1	0.2
1973	0.1	0.1	2.7	1.1	1.1	0.6	0.4	0.7	7.0	7.5	3.4	0.2
1974	0.2	0.1	3.0	1.2	1.1	0.5	0.4	0.6	6.5	7.5	4.1	0.3
1975	0.2	0.1	4.0	1.4	1.3	0.6	0.5	0.7	5.6	6.5	3.0	0.2
1976	0.2	0.1	4.8	1.5	1.3	0.6	0.5	0.8	5.5	6.5	3.3	0.3
1977	0.1	0.1	5.3	1.8	1.4	0.6	0.4	0.6	5.5	6.5	3.8	0.3
1978	0.1	0.1	5.9	1.9	1.4	0.6	0.4	0.6	5.3	6.3	3.9	0.4
1979	0.1	0.1	6.6	2.0	1.5	0.6	0.4	0.6	4.7	5.6	3.8	0.3
1980	0.1	0.1	7.1	1.9	1.5	0.6	0.3	0.5	4.7	5.6	3.9	0.3
1981	0.1	0.1	6.8	1.9	1.6	0.6	0.3	0.5	4.7	5.9	4.6	0.3
1982	0.1	0.1	6.5	1.9	1.6	0.6	0.3	0.5	4.7	5.8	4.8	0.4
1983	0.1	0.1	6.2	1.8	1.5	0.6	0.3	0.5	5.1	6.2	4.9	0.4
1984	0.2	0.1	5.5	1.6	1.4	0.6	0.3	0.4	5.2	6.5	4.1	0.4
1985	0.2	0.1	6.8	1.9	1.4	0.6	0.3	0.5	5.4	7.1	3.9	0.4
1986	0.2	0.1	6.8	1.9	1.4	0.6	0.4	0.5	5.5	6.9	3.5	0.4
1987	0.2	0.1	6.4	1.8	1.4	0.6	0.4	0.4	6.3	7.8	3.4	0.4
Overall rate of change												
1963–87[b]	−0.33	−0.50	3.00	1.00	0.40	0.00	−0.69	−0.60	6.88	12.00	−0.13	1.00
1973–87	1.00	0.00	1.37	0.64	0.27	0.00	0.00	−0.43	−0.10	0.04	0.00	1.00
1980–87	1.00	0.00	−0.10	−0.05	−0.07	0.00	0.33	−0.20	0.34	0.39	−0.13	0.33

Source: Adapted from *Uniform Crime Report* (Washington, D.C.: U.S. Department of Justice, Federal Bureau of Investigation, annual; 1963–1987). Total Arrests, Distribution by Sex.

[a]In 1963, embezzlement and fraud were combined.

[b]For embezzlement and fraud, the rate of change is from 1964 to 1987.

Table 4–9
Rank Order of Offenses for Which Females and Males Were Most Likely to Be Arrested: 1972, 1980, 1987

Rank	1972 Offense	Female[a]	1972 Offense	Male[b]	1980 Female[a]	1980 Offense	Male[b]	1980 Offense	1987 Female[a]	1987 Offense	Male[b]	1987 Offense
1	Larceny/theft	19.1	Drunkenness	21.6	21.2	Larceny/theft	14.5	Drunken driving	20.4	Larceny/theft	14.0	Drunken driving
2	Drunkenness	9.5	Drunken driving	9.5	8.0	Drunken driving	11.9	Drunkenness	8.6	Drunken driving	9.7	Larceny/theft
3	Disorderly conduct	8.0	Disorderly conduct	8.4	7.3	Disorderly conduct	9.8	Larceny/theft	6.4	Drug abuse violations	7.8	Drug abuse violations
4	Narcotic drug law violations	6.3	Larceny/Theft	8.0	7.1	Fraud	7.5	Disorderly conduct	6.3	Drunkenness	7.2	Drunkenness
5	Other assaults	4.0	Narcotic drug law violations	6.1	5.2	Drunkenness	5.6	Drug abuse violations	5.8	Other assaults	6.4	Other assaults
6	Drunken driving	3.9	Burglary	5.0	4.7	Drug abuse violations	5.5	Aggravated assault	5.3	Disorderly conduct	5.5	Disorderly conduct
7	Prostitution	3.1	Other assaults	4.5	4.2	Liquor law violations	4.8	Other assaults	4.7	Liquor law violations	4.7	Liquor law violations
8	Embezzlement and fraud	2.9	Liquor law violations	3.0	4.1	Other assaults	4.4	Liquor law violations	3.4	Burglary	3.9	Burglary
9	Liquor law violations	2.8	Aggravated assault	2.3	3.9	Prostitution and vice	2.8	Prostitution and vice	3.4	Aggravated assault	2.9	Aggravated assault
10	Aggravated assault	2.0	Vandalism	2.0	2.1	Aggravated assault	2.6	Aggravated assault	2.1	Vandalism	2.3	Vandalism

Source: Adapted from *Uniform Crime Report* (Washington, D.C.: U.S. Department of Justice, Federal Bureau of Investigation, annual; 1963–1987). Total Arrests, Distribution by Sex.
[a]Percent arrested out of all female arrests.
[b]Percent arrested out of all male arrests.

Among men, the ordering was even more stable. Except for a decline in the proportion of men arrested for drunkenness and disorderly conduct and an increase in arrests for drunken driving and narcotics, there seem to have been no marked changes. If we combine all alcohol-related offenses, as we did for women, we find an interesting negative trend. These offenses accounted for 34.1 percent of male arrests in 1972, 30.8 percent in 1980, and only 25.9 percent in 1987. Among both men and women, the sharp decrease in arrests for drunkenness and disorderly conduct and the increase in arrests for drunken driving may be as much, or even more, an indication of a shift in police behavior than in the behavior of the men and women arrested.

In sum, the arrest data tell us the following things about women's participation in crime: (1) the proportion of female arrests in 1987 was greater than the proportion of arrests one or two decades earlier; (2) the increase in arrests was greater for serious (Type I) offenses than it was for all Type I and Type II offenses combined. The increase in arrests for serious offenses can be attributed almost entirely to women's greater participation in property offenses, especially larceny. In 1963, roughly 1 out of 5 arrests for larceny involved a woman. Since 1973, the proportion has been approximately 1 out of 3. Contrary to mass media implications, the proportion of female arrests for violent crimes has changed hardly at all over the past two and a half decades, as witnessed by stable female arrest rates for homicide, aggravated assault, and robbery.

Further probing of female arrest rates for Type II offenses revealed that embezzlement, fraud, and forgery/counterfeiting increased the most. None of the other Type I or Type II offenses showed as big a shift as did these three white-collar offenses. Should the rate of change continue, female arrest rates for these offenses will be commensurate with women's representation in society—in other words, roughly equal to male arrest rates—in the next one or two decades. In no category listed in the *UCR* (except prostitution) are women as highly represented.

Among these Type II offenses, however, only fraud accounted for a substantial proportion of females arrested. After larceny, most women, like most men, were arrested for alcohol-related offenses. Contrary to popular media accounts, the majority of female offenders were not arrested for drug law violations. In fact, fraud accounted for as much female crime as did drug law violations in 1987. In this finding, female offenders differed from their male counterparts, whose involvement in fraud was negligible.

One word of caution about interpreting the statistics reported in this chapter: These statistics describe arrests, not known or observed behavior at the scene of a crime. From the arrests, we infer participation in the criminal act. But in discussing women and crime, this inference might not hold because of the discretion available to police and the way in which police may exercise that discretion.

Remember Pollak's argument that the differential rate of crime attributed to men and women was due in large measure to chivalry on the part of law enforcement officials. Indeed, Pollak and other authors might claim that the sharp increase in the percentage of women arrested in the 1970s and 1980s was due to the fact that police have become less chivalrous or less paternalistic and that they are treating women as they would male suspects. Thus, perhaps changes in female crime rates result from changes in the attitudes and behavior of police rather than in the propensities of women to engage in more crimes. However, the fact that the rates of female arrests have varied according to the nature of the offense indicates that the hypothesized change in police behavior cannot account for all of the increases. It is doubtful that police would respond more punitively to female property offenders than to women suspected of killing or assaulting their victims.

Our view is that women are committing fraud, embezzlement, and forgery more often because their participation in the labor force provides them with greater opportunities to commit these offenses than they had in the past. The data in chapter 3 show that the number of women in the labor force increased from 1963 to 1987. They also show that the types of jobs women occupied were likely to provide them with the opportunities to commit fraud, embezzlement, and forgery. During the 1980s, about 70 percent of the women in the labor force were working as bookkeepers, secretaries, salespersons, and management and administrative personnel. They were not in a position to steal hundreds of thousands of dollars, but they were in a position to pocket smaller amounts.

We note in chapter 3 that as of 1980, women headed 10.5 percent of all family households in the United States and 58 percent of those households contained children. Thus, need, as well as opportunity, may account for much of the increased female involvement in property crimes.

Notes

1. Arrests for rape are included in the total arrests for serious crimes and serious violent crimes.
2. National Crime Survey data, which are based on reported victimizations, do provide this information and are thought to give a more accurate account of criminality. However, they were not available until 1973 and thus do not offer enough of a longitudinal perspective.

5
Women in Court

A major question in the study of women in crime is whether the courts treat women differently than they do men. Much of the data collected for the 1980s is examined from that perspective in this chapter. There also have been some procedural changes in the treatment of women. For example, statutes such as the indeterminate sentence for women no longer exist. Also, the procedure whereby a woman's minimum sentence was decided by a parole board in a closed session at which she was not represented by counsel (in contrast to the situation of men, whose minimum sentence has always been determined by a judge at an open hearing and in the presence of counsel) has been abandoned.

As suggested in chapter 1, two schools of thought prevail on how women defendants are treated at the bar of justice. Most observers feel that women receive preferential treatment, which in operational terms means that they are less likely than men to be convicted for the same type of offense; if they are convicted, they are less likely to be sentenced; and if they are sentenced, they are likely to receive milder sentences. The factors thought to motivate judges toward leniency are chivalry and naïveté. For example, judges often say that they cannot help but compare a woman defendant with other women whom they know well—namely, their mothers and wives—and whom they cannot imagine behaving in the manner attributed to the defendant. Practicality also is thought to be a main consideration. Most of the female defendants have young children, and sending the women to prison is thought to place a great burden on the rest of the society.

Paternalism is a particular manifestation of the preferential treatment toward women that many attribute to trial court judges. Nagel and Weitzman (1971) assert that paternalistic behavior has favorable as well as unfavorable consequences for women defendants. The favorable consequences are that women are less likely than men to remain in custody during the pretrial period. Once tried, they are less likely to be convicted; if convicted, they are likely to receive milder sentences. The unfavorable consequences are that women are less likely to have an attorney, a preliminary hearing, or a jury trial.

Using data originally collected by Silverstein (1965) in a national survey of the defense of the poor, Nagel and Weitzman (1971) compared the treatment that men and women charged with assault and larceny received in the courts. Their results are shown in table 5–1. On the basis of these data, Nagel and Weitzman concluded that paternalism prevails almost equally for both types of offenses, except that women are more likely to be jailed in assault cases than in larceny cases. They attribute the different treatment of men and women in assault cases to the fact that assault is a more manly type of crime and that women who commit it pay the price for their behavior by being treated more like men.

The other view about how women fare at the bar of justice is that judges are more punitive toward women. They are more likely to throw the book at a female defendant because they believe that there is a greater discrepancy between her behavior and the behavior expected of a woman than there is between the behavior of a male defendant and the behavior expected of a man. In other words, women defendants pay for the judges' belief that it is more in a man's nature to commit crimes than it is in a woman's nature. Thus, it is maintained, when a judge is convinced that the woman before him has committed a crime, he is more likely to overreact and punish her not only for the specific offense but also for transgressing against his expectations of womanly behavior.

In the past, the existence of statutes such as the indeterminate sentence for women and the sanctioning of a procedure whereby only convicted male defendants had their minimum sentence determined by a judge at an open hearing and in the presence of counsel were cited as evidence of the unfair, punitive treatment accorded women in the court. In an article titled "Discriminatory Sentencing of Women Offenders," Temen (1973) argued for passage of the ERA on the ground that it would make null and void all existing statutes that prescribed longer sentences for female offenders and that permitted only females to receive an indeterminate sentence.[1]

The 1967 opinion of the Superior Court of Pennsylvania on the matter of indeterminate sentences for women [*Commonwealth* v. *Daniel*, 210 Pa. Super. 156, 167, 232, A2d., 247, 253, (1967)] is worth noting:

> This court is of the opinion that the legislature reasonably could have concluded that indeterminate sentences should be imposed on women as a class, allowing the time of incarceration to be matched to the necessary treatment in order to provide more effective rehabilitation. Such a conclusion could be based on the physiological and psychological make-up of women, the type of crime committed by women, the relation to the criminal world, their role in society, their unique vocational skills and their reaction as a class to imprisonment, as well as the number and types of women who are sentenced to imprisonment rather than given suspended sentence.

When the Pennsylvania Supreme Court overruled the lower court's decision, it stated, "While legislative classification on the basis of sex alone did not violate the equal protection clause, it [the court] could find no reasonable justification for a statute which imposed longer sentences on women than on men convicted of the same crime" (430 Pa. at 649, 243, A2d. at 403). The Pennsylvania legislature responded by enacting a law that in essence provided for another type of indeterminate sentence for women. The law stated that only men would have their minimum sentence determined by the court. This procedure entitled a male offender to have his minimum sentence set by a judge at an open hearing during which representation by counsel was constitutionally mandated. A woman's minimum sentence was decided by a parole board during a closed session at which she had no representation or any procedural rights.

The Supreme Court of Pennsylvania declared the act unconstitutional under the state's equal rights amendment and the equal protection clause of the U.S. Constitution. The court also stated that under the reasoning of *Commonwealth* v. *Daniel*, gender-based discrimination in parole eligibility was not permissible (458 Pa. 299, 328 A.2d 857).

In 1973, Debra Anthony conducted twenty-three interviews with judges in Chicago, St. Louis, Milwaukee, and Indianapolis on their experiences with female offenders. She concluded:

> More than half of the Judges said that they do treat women more leniently and more gently than they do men; that they are more inclined to recommend probation rather than imprisonment; and if they sentence a woman, it is usually for a shorter time than if the crime had been committed by a man. Only a small proportion of the Judges said that they were less likely to convict the women. The point at which they differentiate in favor of the women is at the time of passing sentence. (Anthony 1973, 51–52)

Simon and Sharma's 1979 study of criminal processing in Washington, D.C., found little evidence of gender effects on court decisions to dismiss a case, to adjudicate, or to incarcerate (Simon and Sharma 1979). These findings were supported by Kempinen's (1983) study of sentencing decisions in Philadelphia during the 1970s, which found no evidence of gender-based leniency. In a more recent study of criminal processing in Honolulu, Ghali and Chesney-Lind (1986) found that arrested females were more likely than arrested males to be prosecuted and that women were more likely than men to enter a guilty plea for less serious offenses. In later decisions, at the district court level (less severe cases), the findings supported those of Simon and Sharma (1979). No evidence of a gender effect on the court's pretrial dismissal, adjudication, or sentencing decisions was found. At the circuit court level (felonies), there was no evidence of a

Table 5-1
How the Treatment of Female Defendants in Criminal Cases Differs from That of Male Defendants[a]

Case Type and Treatment Stage	Number of Defendants with Available Information		Percent Receiving Treatment		Difference in Percentage Points	Does Paternalism Hypothesis Seem to Be Confirmed?
	Females	Males	Females	Males		
I. Grand Larceny Cases						
A. Being jailed						
1. Released on bail	63	771	76	50	26	Yes
2. Had less than two months' delay of those awaiting trial in jail	10	231	60	67	X	Too few women not released on bail
3. Case dismissed or acquitted	71	841	24	13	11	Yes
4. Received suspended sentence or probation of those convicted	47	656	64	43	21	Yes
5. Received less than one year imprisonment of those imprisoned	9	241	33	45	X	Too few women
B. Formal safeguards						
1. Received preliminary hearing	42	606	57	55	2	Difference too small
2. Had or given a lawyer	61	781	90	87	3	Difference too small
3. Received a jury trial of those tried	18	283	47	31	X	Too few women

II. Felonious assault cases

A. Being jailed						
1. Released on bail	43	615	77	58	19	Yes
2. Had less than two months' delay of those awaiting trial in jail	6	152	17	49	X	Too few women released on bail
3. Case dismissed or acquitted	45	638	36	23	13	Yes
4. Received suspended sentence or probation of those convicted	25	415	44	36	8	Yes
5. Received less than one year imprisonment of those imprisoned	9	172	89	57	X	Too few women imprisoned
B. Formal safeguards						
1. Received preliminary hearing	31	451	74	73	1	Difference too small
2. Had or given a lawyer	42	620	88	89	1	Difference too small
3. Received a jury trial of those tried	24	262	19	45	26	Yes

Source: Adapted from Nagel and Weitzman 1971.

[a]Based on 1,103 grand larceny cases and 846 felonious assault cases from all fifty states for 1962.

gender effect on the court's adjudication decisions, but there was an effect on sentencing. Controlling for legal and social characteristics, females were more likely than males to receive probation.

In 1988, Angela Musolino interviewed twelve judges in the Washington, D.C., metropolitan area and reported that, with one exception, all of them tended "to treat women more gently than they do men" (p. 15). The reasons cited were the responsibility that the women had for the rearing of young children and the way the judges were taught to view women. In the words of one jurist, "I am more lenient toward women, and I've just not been able to grasp why that is, except I love my mother very much" (p. 16). Another observed, "I don't think there's any rational or objective thought about it, but there's a feeling that incarceration for a woman is far more degrading than for a man, and you'll never see them (women) back because they'll do everything they can to keep from going back" (p. 16). Musolino concluded that chivalry, or the theory of preferential treatment for women, received a lot of support at the sentencing stage but not in the determination of guilt or innocence.

In addition to findings about more or less severe punishments, some data suggest that courts differentially invoke legal and extralegal variables in determining punishments among male and female defendants (Fenster 1977; Nagel et al. 1982; and Kruttschnitt 1984). For example, Nagel et al. (1982) found that offense severity was the most important influence on the sentencing of male offenders but that it was not significant in the sentencing of women. In contrast, being married strongly influenced the probability of a woman's being sentenced to prison but had little effect on the decision to incarcerate a man (see also Fenster 1977; Farrington and Morris 1983).

As we might expect, findings of preferential or even differential treatment of female offenders are not without qualifications. As with police arrest decisions, chivalry in the courts is not universal but has been found to be applied selectively within samples of female offenders. For example, in Kruttschnitt's tests of Black's (1976) propositions regarding the behavior of law, she found that women who were "more respectable" and economically better off, as well as women who were more economically dependent (and thus subject to more informal social control), received the least severe court sanctions (Kruttschnitt 1980–1981, 1982). Similarly, several studies have found that family composition has a significant effect on the sentencing of female offenders (Fenster 1977; Nagel et al. 1982; Kruttschnitt 1984; Daly 1987). Married women tended to receive less severe punishments than their single sisters, and women with children were less severely punished than their childless counterparts.

Recent research by Daly (1989a and 1989b) suggests that differences in court sanctioning, both within and between gender groupings, are most dependent on the family status of defendants. In a statistical analysis of court outcomes, she found no evidence of gender-based sentencing disparities among "nonfamilied" men and women, both of whom were sentenced more severely than their "familied" counterparts. In interviews with sentencing judges, she discovered that differentials in sentencing of familied men and women hinged not on judicial chivalry or paternalism, but rather on judicial concern for the care of dependent children:

> The judges' responses suggest that there are concentric circles of judicial protection of children and families that radiate from a central focus on the welfare of children. Effective care-giving labor is the first ring, and economic support, the second. Simultaneously, extant gender divisions of labor place women in the first ring, and men in the second. Therefore, the good family women were viewed as more critical for the maintenance of family life, and the social cost of jailing the family women were seen to be greater. (Daly 1989b, 19)

Daly's findings go beyond the conclusions of other studies of judicial decision making by suggesting that chivalry, or even paternalism, is an inappropriate characterization of the motivational basis for gender differences in the dispensation of courtroom justice. Again, we are directed to consider a female offender's status and role vis-à-vis her family life, as it continues to differ from that of her male counterpart, when examining the factors that propel her into, or shield her from, inclusion in official crime statistics. In doing so, we must again be cautious of theorizing about the universal woman. Given what we know about female prison populations—that they disproportionately comprise poor and minority women, the majority of whom are mothers—we must consider carefully the implications of such findings and wonder about the validity with which judges determine the good family woman from the bad one.[2]

The remainder of this chapter focuses on data that describe rates of convictions and types of sentences received by men and women who are accused of having committed the same type of offense. Unfortunately, there are no comprehensive judicial statistics that describe the relative conviction rates for men and women within each of the state court systems. The state data included in this chapter were obtained by direct solicitations of each of the fifty states requesting any judicial data collected in which the sex of the offender was noted.

Another source of court data is the Administrative Office of the United States Courts, which, since 1963, has published an annual report that describes how defendants are disposed of in the eighty-nine U.S. district courts. These reports contain statistics that describe the proportion of men and women convicted by category of offense.

The following offense categories are included in these reports:

Class I: Fraud, embezzlement, and obscene mail

Class II: Income tax fraud and other fraud

Class III: Liquor and Internal Revenue Service violations

Class IV: Theft, postal fraud, and forgery

Class V: Assault, homicide, border registration of addicts and narcotics violators, and miscellaneous general offenses

Class VI: Counterfeiting, burglary, interstate transportation of stolen property, violations of the Selective Service Act and other national defense laws, and sex offenses

Class VII: Auto theft

Class VIII: Narcotics violations and robbery

As noted in the first edition of this book, the limitations of these data should be obvious, especially after reading the descriptions of the offense categories upon which the statistics are based. Most defendants in the United States, be they males or females, are tried in state courts because they have broken a state law. Thus, the offenses listed represent only a small proportion of all criminal trials.

One purpose these federal statistics may serve is in the comparison of longitudinal trends—that is, the proportions of females who have been convicted in the federal courts from 1963 through 1987. Table 5–2 describes the number and proportion of female defendants who were convicted each year for all of the offense categories combined. Note that from 1980 on, the percentage of females convicted leveled off to about 17 percent, with no sharp increase or decline in the last seven years.

Table 5–3 compares the proportion of convictions of women in selective offense categories between 1964 and 1987. The offense for which the highest proportion of women were convicted was embezzlement. In 1987, 49 percent of all federal convictions were women, and from 1980 on, women accounted for 45 percent or more of all embezzlement convictions in the federal courts. While women were not nearly as visible in other white-collar and property offenses, they made up a greater share of federal offenders convicted of larceny/theft and forgery than they did of those convicted of robbery, assault and homicide, and drug law violations. Consistent with the arrest data, these are the types of offenses most congruent with the theory that as more women enter the labor force and assume positions of trust and authority, female crime rates will increase, especially for embezzlement, fraud, forgery, and theft.

Table 5–2

Number of Males and Females Convicted and Percentage of Females among Convictions in Eighty-nine U.S. District Courts: 1963–1987

	Males Convicted	*Females Convicted*	*Percent Female*
1963	26,914	2,086	7.0
1964	26,228	2,080	7.1
1965	25,975	1,957	6.8
1966	24,528	1,975	7.2
1967	23,766	1,805	6.7
1968	23,069	2,033	7.9
1969	24,060	2,109	7.9
1970	25,203	2,382	8.5
1971	28,581	2,931	9.1
1972	35,160	3,788	9.7
1973	33,126	3,632	9.9
1974	32,643	3,470	9.6
1979	29,247	3,536	10.8
1980	15,931	3,309	17.2
1981	17,892	3,125	14.9
1982	21,702	3,955	15.4
1983	25,398	4,980	16.4
1984	23,651	4,902	17.2
1985	18,795	3,945	17.3
1986	25,202	4,977	16.5
1987	27,277	5,668	17.2
Overall rate of change			
1963–87	0.01	1.72	1.46
1973–87	− 0.18	0.56	0.74
1980–87	0.71	0.71	0.00

Source: Adapted from *Federal Offenders in the U.S. District Courts* (Washington, D.C.: Administration Office of the U.S. Courts, 1963–74; 1979–1987).

Tables 5–4, 5–5, and 5–6 describe the proportion of women convicted by offense categories in the California superior courts from 1966 through 1972 and from 1982 through 1987, the New York lower and upper courts from 1982 through 1987, and all the Pennsylvania trial courts from 1981 through 1986. In the 1980s in these three states, of all the Type I offenses, women contributed the highest percentage to those convicted for theft or larceny. Note also that the percentages were relatively stable during the early 1980s.

Another way of measuring whether women are more or less likely than men to be convicted for the same type of offense is to compare the percentages of prosecutions of women and men that have resulted in convictions for specific offenses. These data are presented in table 5–7 for New York from 1982 through 1987 and in table 5–8 for Pennsylvania from 1981 through 1986.

Table 5–3

Percentage of Females among Convictions by Specific Offense Categories in Eighty-nine U.S. District Courts: 1964–1987

	1964		1965		1966		1967		1968		1969	
	Total	% Female	Total	% Female	Total	% Female	Total	% Female	Total	% Female	Total	% Female
Class I												
Fraud	666	12.4	515	16.7	555	18.9	300	18.7	250	26.4	257	21.8
Embezzlement	1,231	20.7	1,207	19.7	1,148	21.0	1,220	24.5	1,231	24.6	1,421	26.4
Class IV												
Theft[a]	2,418	10.5	2,256	10.8	2,223	9.7	2,137	8.9	2,282	10.6	2,281	9.8
Forgery[b]	1,517	22.4	2,117	21.9	1,958	23.5	1,642	24.1	1,787	24.5	1,441	25.3
Class V												
Assault and homicide	233	8.6	214	8.4	254	2.8	914	12.9	953	9.4	354	7.1
Class VIII												
Narcotics	919	10.6	1,116	10.0	1,052	11.7	914	12.9	953	9.4	1,007	11.9
Robbery	524	3.4	660	2.0	577	5.5	703	2.6	862	3.8	961	4.0

	1970		1971		1972		1973		1974	
	Total	% Female	Total	% Female	Total	% Female	Total	% Female	Total	% Female
Class I										
Fraud	236	33.1	235	28.1	2,203	10.8	2,596	9.8	2,859	10.0
Embezzlement	1,602	27.3	1,940	26.7	1,681	29.2	1,480	28.5	1,494	27.8
Class IV										
Larceny and theft	2,488	10.5	3,088	11.8	3,612	13.5	3,574	13.6	3,280	12.9
Forgery and counterfeiting	1,741	26.3	2,042	27.1	4,429	20.8	3,985	19.4	4,118	20.1
Class V										
Assault and homicide	390	7.4	364	6.0	712	8.3	741	9.4	580	9.3
Class VIII										
Narcotics	919	10.9	1,158	11.3	5,910	10.8	8,538	8.9	8,246	8.6
Robbery	1,002	3.4	1,359	5.3	5,789	9.8	5,669	9.9	4,833	10.3

	1979		1980		1981		1982		1983	
	Total	% Female	Total	% Female	Total	% Female	Total	% Female	Total	% Female
Class I										
Fraud	5,149	13.0	3,667	18.0	3,853	16.5	4,409	19.5	4,991	19.6
Embezzlement	1,652	31.7	1,159	45.5	1,464	44.7	1,878	44.3	1,936	49.0
Class IV										
Larceny and theft	3,919	16.7	2,360	22.3	2,393	16.8	2,479	20.0	3,295	20.5
Forgery and counterfeiting	2,712	21.2	1,633	24.4	1,548	21.5	1,798	23.6	2,348	25.0
Class V										
Assault and homicide	529	6.0	388	8.0	455	10.3	449	10.2	522	9.0
Class VIII										
Narcotics	5,067	8.7	3,824	12.7	4,361	11.7	3,563	12.6	4,396	12.3
Robbery	5,149	13.8	3,288	17.7	3,492	13.1	1,367	5.3	1,333	6.0

	1984		1985		1986		1987	
	Total	% Female	Total	% Female	Total	% Female	Total	% Female
Class I								
Fraud	5,131	20.8	4,081	19.5	5,304	19.1	6,143	19.7
Embezzlement	1,688	49.4	1,366	51.0	1,711	49.0	1,923	48.7
Class IV								
Larceny and theft	3,140	23.9	2,331	23.6	2,632	23.4	2,496	24.0
Forgery and counterfeiting	1,993	26.7	1,590	26.2	1,997	27.0	1,858	28.5
Class V								
Assault and homicide	472	10.6	377	11.4	385	9.4	452	8.8
Class VIII								
Narcotics	4,837	12.8	4,523	14.4	7,189	14.0	8,640	15.2
Robbery	1,220	6.1	1,009	6.9	994	4.9	988	5.7

Source: Adapted from *Federal Offenders in the U.S. District Courts* (Washington, D.C.: Administration Office of the U.S. Courts, 1964–1974; 1979–1987).

[a] From 1964 to 1971, this category was labeled "Theft"; in 1972, it was labeled "Larceny"; in 1973, it was labeled "Larceny and theft."

[b] From 1964 to 1971, this category was labeled, "Forgery"; from 1972 on, it was labeled "Forgery and counterfeiting."

Table 5-4

California: Percentage of Females among Convictions in Superior Courts: 1966–1972 and 1982–1987

	1966		1967		1968		1969		1970		1971		1972	
	Number[a]	% Female	Number	% Female	Number	% Female	Number	% Female	Number	% Female	Number	% Female	Number	% Female
Homicide	656	12.7	764	14.5	851	14.7	731	12.3	850	12.2	940	13.2	1,047	13.8
Robbery	1,666	3.2	2,721	5.0	3,050	4.7	2,106	3.9	2,207	3.1	2,719	3.6	2,753	3.7
Burglary	5,704	3.2	7,691	4.1	8,326	4.4	6,362	3.6	6,499	3.4	7,913	3.4	7,315	3.7
Assault	2,553	8.6	2,650	10.4	3,284	11.0	3,495	10.1	3,373	9.2	3,654	10.3	3,681	9.6
Theft	3,685	16.4	3,563	14.8	3,675	16.7	2,102	13.2	2,410	11.7	2,676	11.1	2,645	9.9
Drug law violations	5,334	9.6	9,877	11.3	12,889	12.0	18,367	12.3	18,672	13.9	20,808	14.4	15,954	14.5

	1982		1983		1984		1985		1986		1987	
	Number	% Female	Number	% Female	Number	% Female	Number	% Female	Number	% Female	Number	% Female
Homicide	1,132	8.6	945	9.2	940	9.1	934	10.8	1,066	9.4	1,027	9.7
Robbery	4,688	5.1	4,389	5.8	4,036	5.4	4,820	4.8	4,723	5.8	4,412	5.9
Burglary	10,038	4.0	9,609	4.5	9,756	5.6	10,513	5.8	10,614	6.1	10,008	6.6
Assault	4,079	8.1	3,789	8.3	3,993	9.0	4,427	8.0	4,750	8.6	4,385	8.1
Theft	7,948	20.6	8,273	22.7	8,838	24.9	10,040	26.1	9,792	24.8	9,476	23.3
Drug law violations	8,454	13.4	10,491	13.5	12,899	13.0	19,763	12.1	26,110	11.9	30,585	12.7

Source: 1966–1972: Adapted from Bureau of Criminal Statistics, *Crime and Delinquency in California* (Sacramento: California Department of Justice, 1966–72); 1982–1987: Unpublished data supplied by Bureau of Criminal Statistics, California Department of Justice, Division of Law Enforcement.

[a]Total number of identified males and females convicted. Number does not include convictions for which gender could not be ascertained.

Table 5-5
New York: Percentage of Females among Convictions in Lower and Upper Courts by Type of Offense: 1982–1987

	1982		1983		1984		1985		1986		1987	
	Number	% Female	Number	% Female	Number	% Female	Number	% Female	Number	% Female	Number	% Female
Homicide	1,984	6.7	1,935	7.0	1,758	6.0	1,681	8.3	1,588	8.2	914	6.5
Robbery	10,347	6.0	12,124	5.7	11,410	5.7	10,706	5.8	11,953	6.4	11,058	7.4
Burglary	21,419	5.3	21,706	5.3	19,513	5.5	18,372	5.1	19,446	5.7	19,735	6.4
Assault	15,490	10.8	15,906	11.2	17,759	10.8	18,561	10.9	18,232	10.4	15,094	10.6
Larceny	38,609	27.1	37,841	27.4	36,096	25.8	37,324	26.4	39,018	26.0	33,505	25.9
Drug law violations	26,667	9.5	30,152	9.9	37,979	10.0	42,428	9.5	50,611	11.5	50,925	12.1

Source: New York Division of Criminal Justice Services, Bureau of Criminal Justice Statistical Services, unpublished data.

aTotal number of identified males and females convicted.

Table 5-6

Pennsylvania: Percentage of Females among Convictions in All Courts by Type of Offense: 1981–1986

	1981		1982		1983		1984		1985		1986	
	Number[a]	% Female	Number	% Female	Number	% Female	Number	% Female	Number	% Female	Number	% Female
Murder	490	11.8	523	10.3	563	11.4	596	12.4	443	10.2	416	10.8
Robbery	2,012	3.0	2,563	4.1	2,294	5.2	2,562	3.8	1,674	3.9	1,734	4.9
Burglary	3,191	2.8	4,661	3.7	4,527	2.9	4,339	3.0	3,325	3.3	3,032	2.8
Aggravated assault	1,836	10.2	1,940	10.8	1,698	11.6	1,741	10.5	1,386	11.2	1,374	10.8
Other assault	3,023	8.8	3,384	9.0	3,927	8.4	3,939	9.1	3,575	9.4	3,695	8.5
Theft	5,419	10.1	10,225	28.9	9,018	24.4	8,499	24.1	7,432	24.6	6,950	24.1
Forgery	906	26.7	816	28.1	897	23.0	940	26.2	850	27.4	971	28.9
Fraud	1,363	29.1	905	25.0	1,307	22.1	1,418	20.8	1,428	28.9	1,559	25.3
Drug law violations	3,592	12.8	3,641	14.2	4,257	15.2	4,464	15.0	4,307	14.4	4,768	13.3

Source: Pennsylvania Commission on Crime and Delinquency: unpublished data.

[a]Total number of identified males and females convicted.

Table 5–7
New York: Percentage of Prosecutions in Upper and Lower Courts Resulting in Convictions by Type of Offense and Sex: 1982–1987

	1982		1983		1984		1985		1986		1987	
	Number	Percent Convicted	Number	Percent Convicted	Number	Percent Convicted	Number	Percent Convicted	Number	Percent Convicted	Number	Percent Convicted
Homicide												
Female	214	61.7	203	67.0	177	59.9	201	69.2	215	60.0	118	50.0
Male	2,732	67.8	2,589	69.5	2,346	70.4	2,180	70.7	2,219	65.7	1,555	55.0
Robbery												
Female	1,059	58.2	1,149	60.0	1,109	58.2	1,164	53.8	1,429	53.7	1,593	51.1
Male	15,301	63.6	17,000	67.3	16,365	65.8	15,958	63.2	17,955	62.3	17,901	57.2
Burglary												
Female	1,818	61.9	1,846	61.8	1,738	62.0	1,623	57.5	1,856	59.4	2,080	60.3
Male	28,043	72.4	27,978	73.5	25,362	72.7	24,327	71.7	25,740	71.3	26,562	69.6
Assault												
Female	3,728	44.8	4,052	44.1	4,307	44.7	4,851	41.8	5,065	37.5	4,536	35.4
Male	27,459	50.3	27,706	51.0	31,407	50.4	32,887	50.3	35,421	46.1	30,754	43.9
Larceny												
Female	15,951	65.7	15,925	65.0	14,806	62.8	15,710	62.8	16,183	62.6	14,072	61.5
Male	40,220	69.9	39,226	70.1	38,488	69.6	39,291	69.9	42,404	68.1	36,716	67.6
Drug law violation												
Female	3,993	63.1	4,560	65.4	5,626	67.6	5,774	69.7	7,494	69.3	8,418	73.3
Male	34,497	70.0	38,165	71.2	47,398	72.1	52,325	73.4	62,384	72.8	60,080	74.5

Source: New York State Division of Criminal Justice Services, Bureau of Statistical Services, unpublished data.

Table 5-8
Pennsylvania: Percentage of Prosecutions Resulting in Convictions by Type of Offense and Sex: 1981–1986

	1981		1982		1983		1984		1985		1986	
	Number	Percent Convicted	Number	Percent Convicted	Number	Percent Convicted	Number	Percent Convicted	Number	Percent Convicted	Number	Percent Convicted
Murder												
Female	98	59.2	76	71.1	91	70.3	98	75.5	62	72.6	67	67.2
Male	656	65.9	613	76.5	637	78.3	666	78.4	511	77.9	512	72.5
Robbery												
Female	159	37.7	215	48.8	205	58.5	207	47.3	217	30.4	233	36.5
Male	3,401	57.4	3,863	63.6	3,318	65.5	3,717	66.3	3,303	48.7	3,359	49.1
Burglary												
Female	242	37.2	315	54.6	212	61.8	232	55.6	243	45.7	194	43.3
Male	5,501	56.4	6,470	69.4	6,055	72.6	5,744	73.3	4,746	67.7	4,477	65.8
Aggravated assault												
Female	711	26.4	594	35.2	517	38.1	541	33.6	587	26.4	592	25.2
Male	5,423	30.4	4,007	43.2	3,304	45.4	3,365	46.3	3,379	36.4	3,562	34.4
Other assault												
Female	1,266	21.1	748	40.8	836	39.4	800	44.8	738	45.7	739	42.5
Male	9,798	28.1	5,709	53.9	6,407	56.2	6,277	57.0	5,601	57.8	6,043	55.9
Theft												
Female	1,441	38.0	4,120	71.8	3,214	68.4	3,095	66.2	2,878	63.5	2,699	62.1
Male	11,254	43.3	12,208	59.5	11,087	61.5	10,581	60.9	8,885	63.1	8,576	61.5
Forgery												
Female	538	45.0	361	63.4	342	60.2	424	58.0	402	58.0	458	61.4
Male	1,269	52.3	891	65.9	909	76.0	991	70.0	946	65.2	1,014	68.0
Fraud												
Female	1,242	32.0	516	43.8	548	52.7	591	49.9	682	60.4	693	56.9
Male	3,082	31.3	1,436	47.3	1,758	57.9	1,873	60.0	1,777	57.2	1,918	60.7
Drug law violations												
Female	1,124	40.7	1,044	49.6	1,137	57.1	1,105	60.5	1,057	58.7	1,073	59.1
Male	7,078	44.3	6,679	46.8	6,320	57.1	6,335	59.9	6,232	59.2	7,183	57.6

Source: Pennsylvania Commission on Crime and Delinquency, unpublished data.

In New York, for every type of offense in each year, a higher percentage of the men who were prosecuted were eventually convicted. The pattern of consistently higher conviction rates for men as opposed to women prevailed in Pennsylvania except for slight reversals among white-collar property offenses such as theft and fraud and drug law violations. Over the five-year time span, there was only a slight difference between the percentages of men and women convicted for drug law violations.

These data support the impressions gained from interviews with judges, who maintain that justice is blind, or almost so, in determining the guilt or innocence of men and women. In chapter 6, we compare punishment by imprisonment for men and women convicted of the same type of offense.

Notes

1. See, for example, *State v. Heitman*, 105 Kan. 139, 181 p. 630 (1919); *Ex parte Dankerton*, 104 Kan. 481, 179 p. 347 (1919); *Platt v. Commonwealth*, 256 Mass. 539, 152 N.E. 914 (1926); *Ex parte Gosselin*, 141 Me. 412, 44 A. 2d 882 (1945), cert. denied sub nom. Gosselin v. Kelley, 328 U.S. 817 (1946); *Ex parte Brady*, 116 Ohio St. 512, 157 N.E. 69 (1927). These cases upheld discriminatory sentencing acts against constitutional challenges.
2. Indeed, Glick and Neto's (1977) study of female prison populations and Lewis and Bressler's (1981) study of the San Francisco jail populations revealed that "black women inmates were far more likely to be living with and responsible for their children than white inmates" (Lewis 1981, 97).

Appendix

Tables 5A–1 through 5A–3 compare the percentages of female arrests in the three states of California, New York, and Pennsylvania, for which we also have conviction data by type of offense for 1982 and 1986. Overall, the comparisons show that for each offense category, the percentage of women who were convicted was about the same or smaller than the percentage of women who were arrested for those same types of offenses. We are not saying that the data compare the same women from the time of their arrest to their appearance in court. The data do indicate that the percentage of women who were convicted for offenses in those categories was no greater than the percentage of women who were arrested in the same years. If the percentage convicted was consistently higher, it would suggest that the courts were acting more punitively toward women. Since it was not, these data are consistent with the interviews and the statistical data reported in chapter 5, which show that there is no evidence to indicate that the courts behaved more punitively toward women than toward men. Indeed, when differences did exist, they were generally on the side of greater leniency toward women.

Table 5A–1

California: Percentage of Females Arrested versus Percentage of Females Convicted among Total Arrests and Convictions by Type of Offense: 1982 and 1987

	1982		1987	
	Arrested	Convicted	Arrested	Convicted
Murder	11.0	8.6	10.2	9.7
Robbery	8.3	5.1	8.4	5.9
Burglary	11.3	4.0	14.3	6.6
Aggravated assault	12.0	8.0	10.9	8.1
Theft	33.1	20.6	33.6	23.3
Drug law violations	14.9	9.6	17.8	12.7

Source: Arrested data were adapted from unpublished data supplied by the U.S. Department of Justice, Federal Bureau of Investigation. Conviction data were adapted from unpublished data supplied by the California Department of Justice, Division of Law Enforcement, Bureau of Criminal Statistics.

Table 5A–2

New York: Percentage of Females Arrested versus Percentage of Females Convicted among Total Arrests and Convictions by Type of Offense: 1982 and 1987

	1982		1987	
	Arrested	*Convicted*	*Arrested*	*Convicted*
Murder	8.3	6.7	6.1	6.5
Robbery	6.2	6.0	8.4	7.4
Burglary	5.2	5.3	6.3	6.4
Aggravated assault	12.1	10.8	14.0	10.6
Larceny	29.3	27.1	29.5	25.9
Drug law violations	9.3	9.5	11.7	12.1

Source: Arrest data were adapted from unpublished data supplied by the U.S. Department of Justice, Federal Bureau of Investigation. Conviction data were adapted from unpublished data supplied by the New York Division of Criminal Justice Services, Bureau of Criminal Justice Statistical Services.

Table 5A–3

Pennsylvania: Percentage of Females Arrested versus Percentage of Females Convicted among Total Arrests and Convictions by Type of Offense: 1982 and 1986

	1982		1986	
	Arrested	*Convicted*	*Arrested*	*Convicted*
Murder	13.4	10.3	13.0	10.8
Robbery	7.3	4.1	8.0	4.9
Burglary	5.0	3.7	6.1	2.8
Aggravated assault	13.4	10.8	13.5	10.8
Other assault	14.2	9.0	13.0	8.5
Theft	27.3	28.9	27.6	24.1
Forgery	31.3	28.1	30.4	28.9
Fraud	40.9	25.0	39.9	25.3
Drug law violations	13.4	14.2	12.4	13.3

Source: Arrest data were adapted from unpublished data supplied by the U.S. Department of Justice, Federal Bureau of Investigation. Conviction data were adapted from unpublished data supplied by the Pennsylvania Commission on Crime and Delinquency.

6
Women in Prison

I n the 1960s, women in prison were referred to as the forgotten offenders by those who wanted to call attention to their plight and to bring about changes in their situation. Part of the reason for the lack of interest in female inmates then and now is that there are so few of them. In 1987, about 22 out of 100 persons arrested for a serious crime was a woman. In the same year, about 10 out of 100 persons convicted of a serious crime was a woman, but only about 5 out of every 100 persons sentenced to a federal or state prison was a woman. As of December 1987, of the approximately 580,000 inmates in state and federal prisons, 29,000 were women. At the present time, there are 5 federal institutions for women, 24 for men, and 7 for both men and women. There are 51 state institutions for women, 536 for men, and 19 that are coed.

Another reason for the lack of interest in female inmates is that the inmates themselves have called so little attention to their situation. Prison reforms—and, indeed, public and official interest in prisoners—are strongly influenced by the amount of disruption and violence that occur inside prisons. Prisoners are likely to receive attention only if they riot, destroy property, endanger the lives of guards and fellow inmates, and submit a list of demands for reforming the institution. Following such activities, the public demands an investigation, the governor appoints a blue-ribbon fact-finding commission, and prison officials acknowledge that reforms may be needed and are likely to be made. During the 1960s and 1970s, a number of serious prison riots occurred in large federal and state institutions. But throughout this period, the number of women's institu-

---

Since the nineteenth century, social reformers, clinicians, and law enforcement officers have been concerned about the physical conditions and facilities under which women inmates must live, the types of educational and vocational training programs available to them, the quality and background of the personnel who supervise them, and the social organization within the prisons. The latter topic has attracted particular attention in the past two or three decades with the publication of works such as Giallombardo's *Society of Women* (1966), Ward and Kassebaum's *Women's Prisons* (1965), and Burkhart's *Women in Prison* (1973). These books, especially the first two, place great emphasis on the informal organization that develops among the inmates and types of obligations and responsibilities, especially sexual, that prisoners develop among themselves. But much of this literature on female inmates while interesting in itself, is not directly relevant to the major issues that this book addresses.

tions that engaged in such behavior was practically nil, and the amount of publicity and interest that such institutions received was proportionate to their failure to call attention to themselves. The 1980s showed no deviation from this pattern among female inmates.

A third reason for the lack of interest in women prisoners is that the crimes women commit usually inconvenience society less than the crimes that men commit. The overwhelming majority of women offenders have not been involved in organized crime, in crimes involving high losses of property, or in crimes that endangered large numbers of people.

Who Are the Women in Prisons?

Table 6–1 shows the percentage of women and men who were sentenced to all the federal and state institutions for selected years from 1971 to 1987. Note that over a period of a decade and a half, the percentage of women in federal prisons ranged from 3.7 to 6.3 percent. In state prisons, in which the bulk of inmates are housed, the percentage of women remained virtually unchanged. These data show that the rate of commitment to prison did not keep up with the rate of female arrests from 1963 to 1987 (that is, an increase in arrests for Type I offenses from 9.4 percent in 1963 to 21.6 percent in 1987). In other words, although a higher percentage of women were arrested for serious offenses, the rate at which they were sentenced to state prisons remained relatively stable.

Going back even further to 1925 (table 6–2), we see that between 1925 and 1979, the aggregate female incarceration rate ranged from 5 to 10 per 100,000 female population compared to the male range of 149 to 264 per 100,000 male population. From 1979 to 1985, there was an increase in the incarceration rates of both men and women, but the increase for men was substantially greater. From 1980 to 1985, the male rate increased from 275 per 100,000 to 394 per 100,000, while the female rate increased from 11 per 100,000 to 17 per 100,000.

Table 6–3 shows the types of institutions to which men and women are committed at the federal and state levels. Note that three times as many men as women have been committed to maximum and closed security institutions at the federal level and twice as many at the state level. In 1988, among the women assigned to maximum security prisons, 15 percent were on death row. Between 1981 and 1988, the percentage of women on death row ranged from 8 percent in 1981 to a high of 17 percent in 1987 (American Correctional Association 1988:xxx).

Table 6–1
Females as a Percentage of All Sentenced Prisoners by Type of Institution: 1971–1987

	Number of Sentenced Prisoners in All Institutions	Percent Female	Percent Female in Federal Institutions	Percent Female in State Institutions
1971	198,061	3.2	3.7	4.7
1972	196,183	3.2	3.7	3.1
1973	204,349	3.3	4.1	3.1
1974	229,721	3.5	4.4	3.2
1975	253,816	3.8	4.6	3.4
1976	262,833	3.8	5.4	3.8
1977	300,024	4.1	5.9	3.7
1978	306,602	4.2	6.2	3.9
1979	314,006	4.2	5.9	3.9
1980	328,695	4.1	5.8	4.0
1981	368,772	4.2	5.6	3.9
1982	414,362	4.3	5.5	4.2
1983	437,238	4.4	5.5	4.3
1984	462,442	4.5	5.8	4.4
1985	503,601	4.6	6.0	4.5
1986	546,659	4.9	6.4	4.7
1987	581,609	5.0	6.3	4.8

Source: U.S. Department of Justice, *Prisoners in State and Federal Institutions* (Washington, D.C.: Bureau of Justice Statistics), annual.

Note: Figures include all inmates sentenced for more than one year.

By and large, however, the types of prisons to which men and women are sent reflect the types of offenses for which they were committed. As the data in tables 6–4 through 6–6 show, the absolute number of women sentenced to prison for homicide was usually less than 125 per year in three of the most populous states—California, New York, and Pennsylvania—from 1981 through 1987. For every year, the data across all three states consistently show that for each type of offense for which men and women were found guilty, men were more likely than women to be sentenced to prison. These results match those reported in the first edition, which looked only at California from 1967 through 1969.

Note also that within each state, the ordering of the types of crimes for which defendants were most likely to receive a prison sentence did not differ noticeably between men and women. The two offenses most likely to receive a prison sentence were homicide and robbery. In Pennsylvania and California, these were followed by burglary; in New York, they were followed by drug violations. In California, there was no difference in the rank ordering for all six

Table 6–2
Prisoners in State and Federal Institutions: Aggregate Incarceration Rates: 1925–1985

Year	Males	Rate	Females	Rate	Year	Males	Rate	Females	Rate
1925[a]	88,231	149	3,438	6	1956	182,190	218	7,375	9
1926	94,287	157	3,704	6	1957	188,113	221	7,301	8
1927	104,983	173	4,363	7	1958	198,208	229	7,435	8
1928	111,836	182	4,554	8	1959	200,469	228	7,636	8
1929	115,876	187	4,620	8	1960	205,265	230	7,688	8
1930	124,785	200	4,668	8	1961	212,268	234	7,881	8
1931	132,638	211	4,444	7	1962	210,823	229	8,007	8
1932	133,573	211	4,424	7	1963	209,538	225	7,745	8
1933	132,520	209	4,290	7	1964	206,632	219	7,704	8
1934	133,769	209	4,547	7	1965	203,327	213	7,568	8
1935	139,278	217	4,902	8	1966	192,703	201	6,951	7
1936	139,990	217	5,048	8	1967	188,661	195	6,235	6
1937	147,375	227	5,366	8	1968	182,102	187	5,812	6
1938	154,826	236	5,459	8	1969	189,413	192	6,594	6
1939	173,143	263	6,675	10	1970	190,794	191	5,635	5
1940[b]	167,345	252	6,361	10	1971[c]	191,732	189	6,329	6
1941	159,228	239	6,211	9	1972	189,823	185	6,269	6
1942	144,167	217	6,217	9	1973	197,523	191	6,004	6
1943	131,054	202	6,166	9	1974	211,077	202	7,389	7
1944	126,350	200	6,106	9	1975	231,918	220	8,675	8
1945	127,609	193	6,040	9	1976	252,794	238	10,039	9
1946	134,075	191	6,004	8	1977[d]	267,097	249	11,044	10
1947	144,739	202	6,343	9	1977	274,244	255	11,212	10
1948	149,739	205	6,238	8	1978	282,813	261	11,583	10
1949	157,663	211	6,086	8	1979	289,465	264	12,005	10
1950	160,309	211	5,814	8	1980	303,643	274	12,331	11
1951	159,610	208	6,070	8	1981	339,375	303	14,298	12
1952	161,994	208	6,239	8	1982	379,075	335	16,441	14
1953	166,909	211	6,670	8	1983	401,870	352	17,476	14
1954	175,907	218	6,994	8	1984	426,713	370	19,395	16
1955	178,655	217	7,125	8	1985	460,210	394	21,406	17

Source: Bureau of Justice Statistics, *State and Federal Prisoners, 1925–1985* (Washington, D.C.: U.S. Department of Justice, 1986).

Note: Incarceration rates are the number of prisoners per 100,000 residential population.

[a]Data for 1925 to 1939 include sentenced prisoners in state and federal prisons and reformatories whether committed for felonies or misdemeanors.

[b]Data for 1940 to 1970 include all adult felons serving sentences in state and federal institutions.

[c]Data for 1971 to present include all adults and youthful offenders sentenced to state or federal correctional institutions whose maximum sentence was more than a year.

[d]Before 1977, only prisoners in the custody of state and federal correctional systems were counted. After 1977, all prisoners under the jurisdiction of state and federal correctional systems were counted. Figures for both custody and jurisdiction are shown for 1977 to facilitate comparisons.

Table 6–3

Adult Inmate Population by Security Level and Sex: June 30, 1988

	Federal Prisons		State Prisons	
	Men	Women	Men	Women
Maximum security				
Number	600	10	98,364	2,173
Percent	1.5	0.4	19.4	9.3
Close security				
Number	9,712	233	48,213	1,565
Percent	24.0	8.4	9.5	6.7
Medium security				
Number	11,012	698	195,178	11,117
Percent	27.2	25.1	38.5	47.4
Minimum security				
Number	14,213	1,613	131,741	7,013
Percent	35.1	58.0	26.0	29.9
Trusty				
Number	0	0	10,263	524
Percent	0.0	0.0	2.0	2.2
Other				
Number	4,994	228	22,906	1,049
Percent	12.3	8.2	4.5	4.5
Total				
Number	40,531	2,782	506,665	23,441
Percent	100.0	100.0	100.0	100.0

Source: American Correctional Association, 1989 *Directory* (Laurel, MD), p. xxv.

Note: Numbers exclude inmates incarcerated in Washington, D.C. (men = 8,292; women = 461) and in Cook County, Illinois (men = 5,696; women = 308).

types of offenses between men and women. The differences that occurred in Pennsylvania and New York were slight and involved assault, burglary, theft, fraud, and drug violations.

Table 6–7 compares the offenses for which men and women were sentenced to all state prisons in 1979 and 1986. In 1986, women represented a smaller percentage of the violent offenders than they did in 1979: 40.7 percent versus 48.9 percent. Of the violent offenses, murder and robbery were most frequently cited for both men and women. Among the property offenses, women were more likely to be committed for fraud and theft than for burglary; men were most likely to be committed for burglary.

Table 6–8 shows the age and education of inmates of federal and state correctional institutions for 1960, 1970, and 1980 as recorded in the Decennial U.S. Census report. Most notable is the increased educational levels of all inmates in custody. By 1980, approximately 27 percent of all male inmates and 22

Table 6–4

California: Persons Convicted in Superior Courts and Sentenced to Prison by Type of Offense and Sex: 1982–1987

	1982		1983		1984		1985		1986		1987	
	Number Convicted	% Sentenced to Prison	Number Convicted	% Sentenced to Prison	Number Convicted	% Sentenced to Prison	Number Convicted	% Sentenced to Prison	Number Convicted	% Sentenced to Prison	Number Convicted	% Sentenced to Prison
Homicide[a]												
Female	97	71.1	87	64.4	86	67.4	101	75.2	100	75.0	100	73.0
Male	1,035	83.2	858	86.7	854	88.8	833	89.9	966	92.3	927	92.3
Robbery												
Female	241	41.1	254	44.5	216	45.8	231	51.9	272	52.2	262	55.7
Male	4,447	64.4	4,135	70.7	3,820	69.9	4,589	70.4	4,451	69.8	4,150	71.3
Burglary												
Female	397	29.5	428	32.2	543	35.7	613	37.8	651	37.5	658	39.7
Male	9,641	41.2	9,181	46.0	9,213	47.5	9,900	49.4	9,963	50.2	9,350	50.7
Assault												
Female	329	17.6	314	18.8	358	21.2	356	19.7	408	14.0	354	22.6
Male	3,750	29.5	3,475	33.3	3,635	34.6	4,071	36.2	4,342	37.5	4,013	38.9
Theft												
Female	1,635	9.8	1,879	13.6	2,200	12.7	2,622	14.8	2,426	19.8	2,206	18.4
Male	6,313	22.3	6,394	25.7	6,638	27.7	7,418	29.4	7,366	31.1	7,270	32.0
Drug law violations												
Female	1,132	7.6	1,417	10.5	1,675	11.2	2,392	10.0	3,115	13.2	3,883	12.5
Male	7,322	14.6	9,074	16.4	11,224	17.2	17,371	17.5	22,995	21.3	26,702	23.3
Total												
Female	3,831	15.4	4,379	17.6	5,078	17.6	6,315	17.8	6,972	20.2	7,463	19.5
Male	32,508	34.7	33,117	36.8	35,384	36.3	44,182	35.2	50,083	35.6	52,412	35.6

Source: California Department of Justice, Division of Law Enforcement, Bureau of Criminal Statistics, unpublished data.

[a]For Homicide, "Percent Sentenced to Prison" includes persons sentenced to death.

Table 6–5

New York: Persons Convicted in Upper Courts and Sentenced to Prison by Type of Offense and Sex: 1982–1987

	1982		1983		1984		1985		1986		1987	
	Number Convicted	% Sentenced to Prison	Number Convicted	% Sentenced to Prison	Number Convicted	% Sentenced to Prison	Number Convicted	% Sentenced to Prison	Number Convicted	% Sentenced to Prison	Number Convicted	% Sentenced to Prison
Homicide												
Female	121	52.9	122	63.9	96	59.4	124	66.1	126	62.7	54	48.1
Male	1,716	78.7	1,650	80.6	1,544	79.5	1,430	78.7	1,387	81.5	778	76.9
Robbery												
Female	279	31.5	349	35.8	340	29.7	311	30.9	415	41.7	417	36.5
Male	6,392	60.5	8,149	60.2	7,378	58.9	6,768	58.8	7,497	59.7	6,900	62.3
Burglary												
Female	208	12.0	212	15.6	217	24.4	174	17.2	205	17.1	203	27.6
Male	6,124	34.7	6,928	39.4	6,009	40.0	5,961	39.7	6,220	42.7	5,854	43.7
Assault												
Female	155	16.8	139	20.1	158	17.7	192	19.3	176	18.2	127	18.1
Male	1,522	30.4	1,522	30.1	1,795	29.8	1,833	31.9	1,740	34.1	1,265	31.6
Larceny												
Female	437	11.4	600	9.5	545	14.7	567	16.6	619	13.1	453	12.1
Male	2,060	23.3	2,310	23.6	2,500	26.8	2,995	27.1	3,147	30.2	2,314	30.8
Drug law violations												
Female	503	16.9	624	19.6	686	19.7	966	21.3	1,440	24.1	1,787	20.6
Male	4,651	37.6	4,823	38.0	5,655	42.7	6,760	41.7	11,219	43.0	12,026	38.1
Total												
Female	1,703	19.8	2,046	21.7	2,042	22.2	2,334	23.4	2,981	25.1	3,041	22.4
Male	22,465	44.7	25,382	46.5	24,881	46.6	25,747	45.4	31,210	46.9	29,137	45.2

Source: New York State Division of Criminal Justice Services, Bureau of Statistical Services, unpublished data.

Table 6-6
Pennsylvania: Persons Convicted in All Courts and Sentenced to Incarceration by Type of Offense and Sex: 1981–1986

	1981		1982		1983		1984		1985		1986	
	Number Convicted	% Incarcerated	Number Convicted	% Incarcerated	Number Convicted	% Incarcerated	Number Convicted	% Incarcerated	Number Convicted	% Incarcerated	Number Convicted	% Incarcerated
Murder												
Female	56	53.6	54	48.1	64	71.9	74	85.1	45	82.2	45	86.7
Male	428	75.9	469	81.9	499	87.6	522	85.1	398	89.7	371	90.0
Robbery												
Female	60	43.3	105	52.4	120	56.7	98	65.3	66	68.2	85	68.2
Male	1,941	74.4	2,456	73.7	2,173	80.1	2,460	83.6	1,608	84.6	1,648	87.0
Burglary												
Female	89	34.8	172	42.4	131	46.6	129	47.3	110	40.0	84	52.4
Male	3,058	62.2	4,486	60.3	4,394	68.9	4,207	73.5	3,212	77.0	2,945	78.1
Aggravated assault												
Female	184	23.4	209	22.0	196	33.7	181	39.2	155	38.1	149	37.6
Male	1,609	40.5	1,725	43.4	1,494	56.0	1,552	60.4	1,231	61.3	1,224	67.3
Other assault												
Female	260	15.4	304	21.1	329	21.0	358	24.9	335	26.3	314	23.2
Male	2,682	29.0	3,077	32.1	3,593	36.7	3,576	38.7	3,227	39.8	3,377	39.7
Theft												
Female	539	18.7	2,947	11.7	2,195	20.0	2,048	21.5	1,822	25.9	1,673	27.2
Male	4,832	35.4	7,243	32.5	6,813	42.5	6,441	44.2	5,599	45.4	5,269	44.5
Forgery												
Female	238	27.7	229	32.8	206	35.4	246	41.1	233	44.6	281	38.1
Male	652	50.9	587	49.9	691	59.8	694	65.4	617	66.1	690	64.5
Fraud												
Female	388	19.8	225	20.0	289	28.4	295	33.6	411	31.1	393	26.2
Male	935	31.3	676	35.5	1,018	38.1	1,123	42.9	1,013	41.9	1,164	41.9
Drug law violations												
Female	455	17.4	517	22.2	649	24.8	669	24.8	619	31.2	634	33.1
Male	3,108	28.3	3,121	31.3	3,606	37.5	3,791	38.6	3,686	40.7	4,133	46.6

Source: Pennsylvania Commission on Crime and Delinquency, unpublished data.

Table 6–7
Offense Distribution of State Prison Inmates by Sex: 1979 and 1986

	Percent of Prison Inmates[a]			
	1979		1986	
	Male	*Female*	*Male*	*Female*
Violent offenses				
Murder	12.2	15.5	11.2	13.0
Negligent manslaughter	3.8	9.8	3.0	6.8
Kidnapping	2.2	1.4	1.7	0.9
Rape	4.5	0.4	4.4	0.2
Other sexual assault	2.0	0.3	4.7	0.9
Robbery	25.6	13.6	21.3	10.6
Assault	7.7	7.6	8.1	7.1
Other violent offenses	0.3	0.4	0.8	1.2
Total	53.3	49.0	55.2	40.7
Property offenses				
Burglary	18.6	5.3	17.0	5.9
Larceny/theft	4.5	11.2	5.6	14.7
Motor vehicle theft	1.5	0.5	1.4	0.5
Arson	0.6	1.2	0.7	1.2
Fraud	3.8	17.3	3.2	17.0
Stolen property	1.3	0.9	2.0	1.6
Other property offenses	0.8	0.4	0.5	0.4
Total	31.2	36.8	30.4	41.3
Drug offenses				
Possession	1.5	2.7	2.9	4.0
Trafficking	4.3	7.1	5.3	7.3
Other drug offenses	0.4	0.7	0.2	0.7
Total	6.2	10.5	8.4	12.0

Source: Adapted from Bureau of Justice Statistics, *Profile of State Prison Inmates* (Washington, D.C.: U.S. Department of Justice, 1986).

[a]Figures do not add up to 100 percent because two offense categories ("Public order offenses" and "Other offenses") were excluded from the table.

percent of all females in federal custody had some college education, compared to only 9 percent of the males and 5 percent of the females in 1960. Data for state inmates show a similar pattern. In 1960, 4 percent of the males an 5 percent of the females had some college education. These percentages jumped to 18 percent of the men and 19 percent of the women in 1980. Almost one-third of all federal and state inmates had completed four years of high school by 1980, as opposed to only about one-seventh in 1960.

Table 6–8

Age and Education of Inmates in Federal and State Correctional Institutions: 1960, 1970, 1980

(percent)

	1960				1970				1980			
	Federal		State		Federal		State		Federal		State	
	Male	Female	Male	Female	Male	Female	Male	Female	Male	Female	Male	Female
Age (years)												
<15	0.0	0.6	0.1	0.1	0.0	0.6	0.3	0.5	0.3	0.3	0.3	0.4
15–19	8.0	7.8	8.6	10.1	3.7	3.8	8.4	11.6	7.6	5.1	7.9	6.1
20–24	20.7	16.0	19.6	17.0	25.4	27.7	26.2	22.8	22.8	21.4	29.9	23.6
25–29	18.5	20.5	18.2	17.7	19.8	23.5	20.3	18.5	22.4	17.4	24.9	25.9
30–39	31.7	31.6	28.5	32.4	27.2	24.0	24.1	24.8	28.3	25.0	24.7	25.8
40–49	13.5	17.1	15.0	14.2	15.3	17.2	13.4	15.4	11.3	9.0	7.9	9.2
50–64	6.9	6.3	8.7	7.5	7.6	3.3	6.2	4.5	6.3	4.6	3.9	5.7
65+	0.7	0.0	1.4	0.9	1.0	0.0	1.0	1.9	1.0	17.2	0.5	3.3
Education (years)												
Elementary												
0–4	10.4	10.1	16.6	14.2	6.3	6.4	7.9	5.8	3.7	4.6	3.9	4.8
5–8	39.4	46.7	41.8	39.8	30.9	24.9	33.8	29.6	14.5	18.7	17.7	15.1
High school												
1–3	26.8	25.0	27.2	28.9	33.9	38.6	34.3	37.4	22.2	25.6	30.1	29.1
4	14.8	13.8	10.6	12.3	20.3	21.8	18.6	20.1	32.6	29.1	29.9	31.8
College												
1–3	7.0	3.3	3.1	3.8	6.1	6.0	4.6	5.6	18.3	14.6	15.1	15.5
4+	1.7	1.2	0.8	1.0	2.4	2.3	0.8	1.5	8.7	7.3	3.3	3.7

Source: U.S. Bureau of the Census, 1960 Decennial Census, *Characteristics of Persons under Custody in Correctional Institutions,* tables 4 and 25; 1970 Decennial Census, *Persons in Institutions and Other Group Quarters,* tables 3 and 24; 1980 Decennial Census, *Persons in Institutional and Other Group Quarters,* table 14.

Table 6–9
Occupational Status of Inmates in Federal and State Correctional Institutions: 1960, 1970, 1980[a]

(percent)

	1960 Federal		1960 State		1970 Federal		1970 State		1980 Federal		1980 State	
	Male	Female	Male	Female	Male	Female	Male	Female	Male	Female	Male	Female
Total with occupation[a,b,c]	75.0	56.5	61.4	44.8	72.1	57.3	67.6	65.8	72.5	54.8	66.2	61.1
Never worked	4.5	11.5	3.9	12.9	7.1	9.0	7.3	18.6	8.5	21.9	11.8	20.1
No occupational information[d]	20.6	31.9	34.7	42.3	20.8	33.6	25.0	15.6	19.0	23.3	22.0	18.8
Occupation Type												
White collar												
Professional, technical, or administrative	9.1	6.0	3.8	4.4	12.8	17.9	5.8	5.3	9.2	13.2	6.2	11.4
Clerical	4.8	14.8	2.7	10.0	4.7	21.9	5.1	18.5	4.9	7.1	3.8	8.8
Sales	4.8	8.1	2.3	2.9	6.4	5.4	2.5	4.1	5.6	24.1	4.4	18.0
Total	18.7	28.9	8.8	17.3	24.0	45.2	13.4	27.9	19.7	44.4	14.4	38.2
Blue collar												
Craft	18.7	3.8	12.9	0.4	18.9	0.0	21.3	2.9	20.6	6.5	22.8	3.7
Operatives/laborers[e]	35.1	20.0	39.3	18.6	41.5	14.0	48.5	24.2	37.6	15.3	40.5	21.6
Service[f]	9.5	36.0	8.3	49.7	10.4	39.6	12.7	41.7	14.7	28.2	15.1	32.9
Farming, forestry, or fishing[g]	6.2	2.5	6.5	2.6	5.2	1.2	4.1	3.3	7.3	5.5	7.3	3.6
Total	69.5	62.3	67.0	71.3	76.0	54.8	86.6	72.1	80.2	55.5	85.7	61.8
No occupation reported	11.9	8.8	24.2	11.4	—	—	—	—	—	—	—	—

Source: U.S. Bureau of the Census, 1960 Decennial Census, *Characteristics of Persons under Custody in Correctional Institutions*, table 25; 1970 Decennial Census, *Persons in Institutions and Other Group Quarters*, table 24; 1980 Decennial Census, *Persons in Institutional and Other Group Quarters*, table 14.

[a]Figures are not strictly comparable across years due to changes in occupational categorizations.

[b]For 1960 and 1970, totals include inmates fourteen years and older, but for 1980, totals include inmates sixteen years and older.

[c]For 1960, figures indicate the number of inmates who reported last working in 1950 or later; for 1970, 1960 or later; and for 1980, 1975 or later.

[d]Included in this category are inmates who last worked in 1959 or earlier and those who did not report the last year that they worked. For 1980, figures include inmates who had been employed in the armed services.

[e]Includes all nonfarm laborers and operatives.

[f]Includes private household workers.

[g]Includes all farm-related occupations, including farm owners and managers as well as laborers.

The age distribution of inmates has not changed much over the years, except perhaps for a slight shift from a smaller percentage of male and female inmates in the 30- to 39-year-old range and a larger percentage in the 20- to 24-year-old range.

Table 6–9 examines the occupational backgrounds of men and women in federal and state custody. We see that the number of incarcerated women who reported never having worked increased over the years, but with the high percentage of absence of information about work histories, it is difficult to make too much of that trend. We also see that among women for whom there are occupational data, the percentage reporting a white-collar occupation—especially in the professional, technical, and administrative category—increased, while the percentage reporting a blue-collar occupation declined. Although this trend seems to be reversed for the men, we cannot be certain because of the number not reporting their occupational category.

Inside Women's Prisons

The U.S. prison system has been a target of the equal rights movement because it continues to provide separate facilities for men and women. Separate prisons were established for women beginning in the 1880s as a reform intended to give them the benefit of rehabilitation then being sought for young men and boys in new reformatories (Singer 1973).

Writing in 1975, Simon said that with the exception of Pennsylvania, Florida, Mississippi, and New Mexico, every state segregated their male and female prisoners by housing them in separate facilities. Those four states maintained men and women in separate wings of the same institutions and segregated them within daily activities. Advocates of the ERA claimed that the same reasoning that was persuasive to the Supreme Court in *Brown* v. *the Board of Education* (that segregation by itself denies to blacks equal experiences) should apply to women because of the maintenance of a separate prison system. By definition, schools that segregate by race and prisons that segregate by sex are basically discriminatory.

In a note published in the *Yale Law Journal* Arditi et al. (1973) claimed that although the Supreme Court had not yet made the same determination concerning segregation on the basis of sex as it had concerning segregation on the basis of color (separate, by its nature, cannot be equal), the passage of the ERA would compel such a result. As of 1989, there were nineteen coed prisons in the state system located in eleven states and seven coed institutions in the federal system.

The fact that women prisoners make up only 5 percent of all prisoners continues to influence the conditions of their incarceration in many important ways. Indeed, the effect begins from the moment a woman is sentenced. Because there are fewer female institutions, she is likely to be sent much farther away from her community than is her male counterpart. Few states operate more than one female penal institution. Women inmates thus experience greater difficulty in keeping track of their families and their possessions. In a letter from the superintendent at the California Institution for Women she characterized the situation as follows:

> Almost all the women who come to prison have husbands and children. If a man goes to prison, the wife stays home and he usually has his family to return to and the household is there when he gets out. But women generally don't have family support from the outside. Very few men are going to sit around and take care of the children and be there when she gets back. So— to send a women to prison means you are virtually going to disrupt her family. She knows that when she gets out she probably won't have a husband waiting for her. It will really mean starting her life over again.

It is also more difficult for a woman to communicate with her lawyer and to gain access to the parole board.

The size of the female prison population also affects the heterogeneity of the population within women's prisons. Women's prisons contain a more heterogeneous population than do men's prisons. They include a wider range of ages, and there is less differentiation by type of offender. All but five states have more than one institution for male offenders, and the decision about which type of institution to commit an offender to is based on age and type of offense.

Not all of the differences between men's and women's institutions result in women experiencing more negative treatment. The stereotypes of women popular in American society provide some advantages to female inmates:

> Women just weren't considered as dangerous or as violent as men. So—rather than the mass penitentiary housing used for men—women's prisons were designed as a domestic model—with each women having a "room" of her own. Often no more stretches of open fields or wire fences separate women prisoners and the "free world"—armed guards are rarely visible. Just like women outside, a woman prisoner would be confined to "the home."
> "The home" planned for women was a cottage that was built to house 20 to 30 women—who would cook their own food in a "cottage kitchen." The cottages in most states were built to contain a living room, a dining room, and 1 or 2 small reading rooms. (Burkhart 1973, 367)

Physically, then, female institutions are usually more attractive and more pleasant than the security-oriented institutions for men. They tend to be located in more pastoral settings, and they tend not to have the gun towers, concrete walls, and barbed wire that so often characterize male institutions. Women inmates usually have more privacy than men inmates; they tend to have single rooms; they may wear street clothes rather than prison uniforms; they may decorate their rooms with bedspreads and curtains provided by the prison. Toilet and shower facilities also reflect a greater concern for women's privacy. Because women prisoners are perceived as less dangerous and less prone to escape than men, most states also allow them more trips outside the prison.

In the first edition of this book, Simon noted that one of the major sources of criticism of women's prisons was the quality and variety of the educational and vocational training programs available in those institutions. For example, based on a survey conducted among inmates in two of the three federal prisons for women, the Women's Bureau of the Department of Labor concluded that 85 percent of the inmates wanted more job training and 80 percent wanted more educational opportunities than were available at those institutions (Koontz 1971, 7). Nine out of 10 of the respondents also said that they expected to work to support themselves when they were released. A majority also expected that they would support others who were dependent on them.

A survey by Arditi et al. (1973) showed that the average number of programs in men's prisons was 10, compared to 2.7 in women's prisons. Whereas male prisoners had a choice of some 50 different vocational programs, the women's choices were limited to cosmetology, clerical training, food services, serving, IBM keypunching, and training as nurse's aides. Some of the men's prisons provided vocational training in programs that were available to women inmates as well, but none of the prisons for women were prepared to train their inmates in programs that were available to men.

The industries available at men's and women's institutions showed much the same picture. In the forty-seven prisons for men, there was an average of 3.2 industries, as compared to 1.2 in the fifteen female prisons. There was also very little overlap concerning the types of industries in which both male and female inmates could work. According to Burkhart (1973), both male and female prisoners were still employed in the personal service of prison administrators. Women prisoners often worked as housemaids and cooks for the families of prison superintendents.

By 1980, a General Accounting Office (GAO) report to Congress denied that gender equality had made headway within prison walls. The title of the report, "Women in Prison: Inequitable Treatment Requires Action," served as an appropriate indicator of its general message. That the type and variety of programs, services, and opportunities for women in prison had not reached parity with those provided to men in prison was attributed to long-standing factors such as the following: (1) the small numbers of women incarcerated, (2) cost, and (3) attitudes among correctional officials who "maintain[ed] a traditional view toward the training programs and other vocational needs of women offenders" (U.S. Comptroller General 1980, 22). In other words, little had changed.

Indeed, gender equality within prisons has been the subject of a considerable amount of state and federal litigation, much of it successful—in edict if not in practice. By 1983, there was active litigation regarding educational programs for women in at least thirteen states, regarding vocational programs in at least twelve states, and regarding prison industries in at least eight states (Ryan 1984).

Since 1975, at least two comprehensive national studies of services, programs, and work opportunities available to female inmates have been conducted—one in 1975 (Glick and Neto 1977) and the other in 1983 (Ryan 1984). Summarizing the historical perspective achieved by comparing these two studies, Ryan (1984) notes:

> ABE [Adult Basic Education] programs have increased by 23 percent, GED/ high school diploma programs have increased by 21 percent and college programs have increased by 19 percent. In 1975, correctional institutions reported offering one to nine vocational programs, with clerical skills, cosmetology, and food services the most common. In 1983, correctional institutions reported offering from one to 13 programs with clerical skills/business education the most common, followed by food services and cosmetology. . . . The study by Glick and Neto (1977) did not report on prison industries. In 1983, it was found that 53 percent of the facilities responding had prison industries, with one to three industries. (p. 28)

In 1984, the Federal Bureau of Prisons became the target of a class-action suit representing the claims of two thousand minimum security female inmates charging discriminatory treatment in the type and quality of facilities in which they were being housed.[1] Specifically, in contrast to minimum security male inmates who traditionally are housed in small, relatively open camps, at cushy "Club Feds," or at military installations, minimum security women have been housed in full-scale prisons offering fewer amenities and freedoms, often being subject to much more stringent security conditions. While to date this suit has been successful in pressuring the Bureau of Prisons into opening three minimum security camps for women, it has not yet resolved claims that the women's camps do not offer comparable educational, employment, or recreational opportunities and that the special medical needs of women and those of women with children are not adequately addressed (Kornhauser 1989).

Survey of State Institutions

To assess the current state of vocational training and work opportunities provided to incarcerated women, we conducted a survey of forty state-run institutions for women listed in the 1988 *American Correctional Association Directory
of Institutions*. Our selection of institutions excluded community-based programs, prerelease or work-release programs, and co-correctional facilities.
Thirty-seven of the forty facilities (93 percent) completed the survey.

Vocational Programs

Perhaps the most interesting finding was the increase in the number of vocational
programs available for women since the survey reported by Arditi et al. (1973).
Unfortunately, the gains were not uniform across state institutions. The 1989
survey showed that the number of vocational programs within a given institution ranged from one to twenty-five and that training was available in approximately seventy different vocations.

The tendency to train women prisoners in skills that reinforce either the
traditional role of wife and mother or the sex segregation of the labor market
that has been identified in earlier studies (Arditi et al. 1973; Glick and Neto
1977; Chapman 1980; Ryan 1984) is still the norm. Seventy-six percent (twenty-
eight) of the responding institutions provided clerical/office skills training; 68
percent (twenty-five) provided typing; 51 percent (nineteen) provided data processing; 46 percent (seventeen) provided cooking and other domestic skills such
as housekeeping and laundry; 40 percent (sixteen) provided food service and
cosmetology; and 35 percent (thirteen) provided bookkeeping, garment manufacturing, and nurse's aide training.[2] The following are examples of less sex-
typed programs offered by a number of the institutions surveyed: 38 percent
(fourteen) offered training in computer programming and building maintenance;
27 percent (ten) provided training in building trades; 24 percent (nine) provided
training in carpentry and plumbing; 22 percent (eight) provided training in
graphics and painting; 19 percent (seven) provided training in printing and welding; and 16 percent (six) provided training in brick masonry and electronics.

Table 6–10 illustrates comparative changes among vocational training of-
ferings for a selected group of institutions. The institutions were selected on the
basis of two criteria: (1) their inclusion in the 1973 Arditi et al. study, and (2)
their response to our survey. The comparison shows that while some state facilities have made great improvements in the breadth and focus of their vocational

training programs, many still provide minimal opportunities or opportunities that are modeled on the traditional female role. As such, they provide the women with little training for facilitating their economic independence either from men or from crime.

Industries

The 1989 survey showed substantial variation in the number and types of prison industries available for women prisoners in state institutions, although the range of industries was much more restricted than the range of vocational programs. Among the thirty-seven institutions responding, 86 percent had at least one industry. The number of industries within a given institution ranged from zero to nine. Overall, twenty-six different types of industries were available to women prisoners in the responding institutions. The three most frequently cited industries were data processing in 41 percent (fifteen) of the institutions, garment manufacturing in 35 percent (thirteen) of the institutions, and laundry in 27 percent (ten) of the institutions. These industries were followed in frequency by food service in 19 percent (seven) of the institutions, upholstery in 16 percent (six) of the institutions, and printing in 14 percent (five) of the institutions. Five, or 14 percent, of the responding institutions reported having no industries. Table 6–11 compares the results of the 1989 sample with those of Arditi et al. (1973).

The data collected by the 1989 survey do not clearly define the quality of the training and/or work experience provided by the responding institutions or its meaningfulness to the offender once she is released from prison. Some authors have suggested that what is termed vocational training or industry work is in reality a work assignment, the goal of which is institutional maintenance (see, for example, Mann 1984). Such work assignments may amount to little more than unskilled domestic work that fails to prepare women for the public job market upon their release. Glick and Neto (1977) documented the customary use of female prisoners to provide domestic services to prison administrators and state officials. One must question the value of vocational programs or industries in cooking, food service, housekeeping, and laundry. Even the valid industrial work that is available, such as data processing and garment manufacturing, may be useless in providing women with skills that they need to secure jobs in such industries on the outside. For example, Glick and Neto (1977) found that garment industry training provided to prisoners was technologically useless due to outdated machinery available in the prisons, suggesting that caution should be used in interpreting our data in an overly optimistic manner.

Table 6-10
Vocational Programs at Selected Women's State Correctional Facilities Revisited

	Tutwiler (Alabama)	California Correction Facility	Connecticut Correction Facility	Indiana Women's Prison	Minnesota Correction Center	Missouri Correction Center	Bedford Hills (New York)	Washington Correction Center
Air-conditioning repair					1			
Arts and crafts		1	1	1		1	1	
Autobody repair								1
Baking			1					
Bookbinding	1	1	1	1		1	1	
Brick masonry		1		1			1	
Building maintenance	1	1		1			1	
Building trades	1			1				
Business machines				1				
Cabinetmaking								1
Canine training				1		1		
Carpentry								
Carpet laying					1			2
Clerical	1	1		2	1	2	1	
Computer maintenance	1	1				1	1	
Computer programming			1			1	1	
Cooking			1	2		2	2	
Cosmetology	2	1	1	1	1	1	1	
Data processing	1	1		1		1		1
Dental technician								
Drafting			1	1				1
Electrical		1	1			1	1	
Electronics		1	1			1		
Engine and appliance repair			1			1		
Farm equipment repair				1				

Farming	2					
Floral design	1					
Food service	2	1		0	1	2
Garment manufacturing	1			2	1	1
Graphics	1	1		1		
Home economics[a]						
Horticulture		1				
Housekeeping	0					1
Janitorial		1				
Laundry		1				
Leather work		1			1	
Machine shop		1				
Metalwork		1		1	1	
Nursery school						
Nurse's aide	1	1	1	1	1	
Office machine repair		1		1		
Oil burner repair		1				
Optics						
Painting	1	1	1		1	
Plumbing	1	1	1		1	1
Printing	1	1				
Radio/TV repair		1			1	
Receptionist aide					1	
Silk screening					1	
Steam fitting						
Tailoring		1	1			1
Typing	1	1	1	1	1	
Upholstering	1	1		1		
Welding	1	1		1		
Word processing	1	1				

Note: 0 = a vocational program that was reported in 1973 but not in 1988; 1 = a vocational program that was reported in 1988 but not in 1973; 2 = a vocational program that was reported in both 1973 and 1988.
[a]Home economics includes training in nutrition and consumer education.

Table 6-11

Industries at Selected Women's Correctional Facilities Revisited

	Tutwiler (Alabama)	California Correction Facility	Connecticut Correction Facility	Indiana Women's Prison	Minnesota Correction Center	Missouri Correction Center	Bedford Hills (New York)	Washington Correction Center
Auto repair	0	1						
Canning								
Cloth maintenance	1							1
Data processing		1	1		1			
Dental						1		
Farming								1
Flag manufacturing					1			
Food service							0	
Garment manufacturing	0	2					0	
Laundry	2	1		2	1		0	
Library								
License plate making								
Machine shop		1						
Metal shop		1						
Printing		1			1			
Shoe manufacturing					1			
Tailoring								
Upholstery		1						

Note: 0 = a vocational program that was reported in 1973 but not in 1988; 1 = a vocational program that was reported in 1988 but not in 1973; 2 = a vocational program that was reported in both 1973 and 1988.

Education

Just as women outside of prison have made their most visible social gains in the area of education, so too have women inside prison walls. According to our survey, both basic and advanced educational opportunities for women in prison are uniformly available. Of the thirty-seven institutions that responded, 97 percent (thirty-six) offered elementary reading and writing, 84 percent (thirty-one) offered elementary arithmetic, and 87 percent (thirty-two) offered a general grade-school curriculum. In all the institutions, general equivalency diploma (GED) preparation was available, and all but one offered college-level courses, often in conjunction with local colleges or universities. Eight percent (three) offered postgraduate courses.

Facilities for Young Children

Considering statistics estimating that between 56 and 75 percent of incarcerated women have young children, the number of institutions accommodating the special needs of mothers with children are disproportionately low.[4] Only 35 percent (thirteen) of the responding institutions reported having either "rooms with cribs, high chairs, or other 'baby' equipment,'" or "rooms to talk privately, read, listen to music with older children," and only 50 percent (nineteen) of the responding institutions reported having "rooms with toys and other facilities for children up to 6 years of age." Even fewer, 30 percent (eleven), reported having "places to prepare food for children."

Not surprisingly, we also found a great disparity among the institutions in the amount of time allowed for mother-child visitation. Seven of the thirty-seven institutions allowed visitation seven days a week. These institutions, representing five state correctional systems, are Bedford Hills Correctional Facility in New York, Albion Correctional Facility in New York, Huron Valley Women's Facility in Missouri, Florence Crane Women's Facility in Missouri, Oregon Women's Correctional Facility, Pennsylvania State Correctional Institution, and Wyoming Women's Center. Eleven of the facilities permitted visitation once a week (with the number of hours allowed during this visit ranging anywhere from one hour to ten hours), three permitted it two times a month, and another two permitted it only once a month.

More than half (nineteen) of the institutions responding reported that they had a furlough program whereby mothers could visit their children at home or in halfway houses. Most often, however, these programs had stringent eligibility requirements and were available only to offenders on work release, those convicted of relatively minor crimes, or those within sight of their release dates.

Survey of Federal Institutions

As of the summer of 1989, the Federal Bureau of Prisons reported housing a total of 3,629 women in twelve federal facilities and in five state facilities that contracted to accept female inmates from the federal system. Of the twelve federal facilities housing women, five accepted only women, while the other seven accepted both women and men. Together, the five federal facilities that accepted only women housed approximately 73.3 percent of all incarcerated female federal prisoners. These facilities included two federal correctional institutions—one located in Alderson, West Virginia, and another in Lexington, Kentucky—which together housed approximately 59.1 percent of all women incarcerated in the federal system. The other exclusively female facilities included three federal prison camps located in Danbury, Connecticut; Marianna, Florida; and Phoenix, Arizona. These institutions collectively housed approximately 14.2 percent of federal women prisoners.

How does the federal system compare to the state system in terms of vocational training, education, and child visitation? Focusing on the five federal facilities exclusively housing women, we administered the same survey given to the exclusively female state facilities. Given the small number of federal facilities, we cannot report the results in a manner that is strictly comparable to the results of the state survey. We can, however, make some generalizations. Remember that the results of the federal survey must be interpreted in the context of pending litigation (Butler v. Thornburgh) that could render them obsolete.

With regard to vocational programs, it appears that only the two correctional institutions—Alderson and Lexington—actually provided exposure to vocational skills in a manner that suggests an educational component. The federal camps, however, indicated that their responses to vocational program items were based on the existence of job assignments in the various skill areas. Not surprisingly, then, we found that the most prevalent vocational skills listed were those contributing to the upkeep and functioning of the institution. All three camps indicated that they offered vocational skills through work assignments in building maintenance, clerical offices, food service, housekeeping, and laundry.

As in the state systems, there was quite a bit of variation among the institutions regarding the types of skills to which inmates were exposed, either through actual training or job assignment, as shown in table 6–12. At least two facilities indicated training or job assignments in the following areas: arts and crafts, baking, brick masonry, carpentry, cooking, dental technology, drafting, horticulture, landscaping, painting, plumbing, printing, recreational aid, and welding. At least one facility reported training or work in air-conditioning repair, auto mechanics, business office skills, commissary work, computer program-

Table 6–12
Vocational Skills Training Offered in Federal Women's Prisons: 1989

	Alderson	Lexington	Danbury	Marianna	Phoenix
Air-conditioning repair	X				
Arts and crafts			EC	X	RI
Auto mechanics	X				
Baking		AP	JA		
Brick masonry	X		JA		
Building maintenance			JA	JA	JA
Building trades	X	X	JA	JA	
Business office skills		X			
Carpentry	X		JA		
Clerical			JA	JA	JA
Commissary				JA	
Computer applications					X
Computer programming			EC		
Cooking	X	AP			JA
Data processing	X				
Dental technology	X	AP			
Drafting		AP	JA		
Food service			JA	JA	JA
Garage work				JA	
Graphics			JA		
Horticulture		X	JA		
Housekeeping				JA	JA
Landscaping	X			JA	
Laundry			JA	JA	JA
Machine shop		AP			
Painting	X	AP	JA		
Plumbing	X	AP			
Printing	X	AP			
Recreation aid			JA		JA
Steam fitting		AP			
Typing			EC		
Welding	X	AP		JA	

Note: EC = enrichment class; X = Vocational Training Program; RI = recreational instruction; AP = apprentice program; JA = job assignment.

ming, data processing, graphics, garage work, machine shop, steam fitting, and typing.

In contrast, within the entire federal system, there was little variety in the number and types of industries reportedly available for federal female inmates. As table 6–13 indicates, among the five institutions, only seven industries were represented. Each institution reported having two industries, with the exception of Lexington, which reported having three industries.

Table 6–13
Industries in Federal Women's Prisons: 1989

	Alderson	Lexington	Danbury	Marianna	Phoenix
Cable manufacturing		X			
Data processing		X		X	
Electronic cable distribution					X
Garment manufacturing	X				
Printing	X	X			
Shipping and receiving/ packaging and procurement			X		X
Warehousing			X	X	

Note: X = Industries Available.

As with the state facilities, the federal facilities were fairly uniform in the provision of educational opportunities for women. All five of the facilities reported having both grade-school and high-school curriculums, and four reported some level of postsecondary-school education.

Child visitation is more problematic in the federal system than it is in the state system because only a small number of facilities serve the population of female offenders. While there may be only one facility within a state that houses female offenders, women adjudicated under the federal system are more likely to be incarcerated outside of their home states. Once in the federal system, an inmate may be housed in any federal facility throughout the country. This situation has obvious negative implications for the continuity of family life, for both men and women. It is particularly salient for women when one recalls that a large majority of all the women incarcerated in the federal system reside in just two institutions, Alderson and Lexington. Thus, we must keep this geographic reality in mind to qualify our examination of the child care facilities provided by the federal women's institutions.

All the facilities said that they provide rooms with toys and other conveniences for children up to six years of age. Alderson and Lexington appear to have more uniform and comprehensive provisions—in terms of both facilities and time—for child visitation than do the prison camps, but they also may have larger numbers of inmates whose families cannot take advantage of such provisions. All the federal facilities reported having furlough programs for eligible mothers, and the survey responses suggested that they are somewhat more liberal than those offered at the state level. In at least two of the facilities, an inmate may become eligible within two years of release, and at least one other said that it allows eligibility within one year of release.

Conclusion

Women make up about 6 percent of all inmates in federal prisons and about 5 percent of all inmates in state institutions. These figures remained relatively stable from 1970 to 1990. While the female incarceration rate rose in the 1980s, it did not increase nearly as much as the male incarceration rate. Women were much more likely than men to be assigned to medium and minimum security institutions at both the federal and state levels. The types of offenses for which women were most likely to receive prison sentences were fraud, larceny, homicide, robbery, and drug violations.

A big improvement has occurred between 1973 and 1989 in the academic programs and in the facilities that were available for contact and visits with female inmates' children. Vocational training programs and job opportunities also increased for female inmates. While these programs and jobs tend to perpetuate female stereotypes, they do provide women with some opportunities to earn money and to acquire some employable skills.

Notes

1. The case, *Butler v. Meese*, is still pending and is now called *Butler v. Thornburgh*.
2. Fifty-one percent (nineteen) of the institutions indicated that they provided vocational training in arts and crafts, but one must wonder whether this training is more recreational than vocational.
3. See Feinman (1986), who cites Glick and Neto (1977) as finding 56.3 percent with one or more children. Feinman (1976) found that 75 percent of women inmates had one or more children. Baunach (1979) found that 70.4 percent of inmates had one or more children. McGowan and Blumenthal (1978) wrote that on any given day, 70 percent of the women in prisons and jails were mothers.

Epilogue

In the fifteen years since the first edition of this book was published, women and crime has become a major intellectual and professional specialty. Within criminology and criminal justice, and among the subfields within sociology, psychology, and economics, research on women who commit crimes has grown into a major area of interest.

In this edition, we have brought up to date the demographic data and the arrest, conviction, and prison statistics reported in the first edition. Overall, the trends are consistent. Women's participation in the labor force has not abated; indeed, a higher percentage of women—including those who are married and have preschool children—than ever before are working full-time. Not only are more women working outside their homes, but they are occupying positions in the labor force that involve more training, responsibility, and authority than they had in the past. Along with women's greater participation in the labor force, promotion to higher-status positions, and increased representation in the professions, there is also a higher percentage of female-headed households in which women are the caretakers of young children.

With these data as background for understanding the position of women in American society, we turned to the female crime statistics and examined trends in these data. The findings were not dramatic, but the pattern we saw forming in the late 1960s and early 1970s has continued. Women's participation in property and white-collar crimes has continued to increase. In 1987, 31 percent of all larceny, 44 percent of all fraud, 34 percent of all forgery, and 38 percent of all embezzlement arrests were of women offenders. The percentages of women arrested for robbery (8 percent) and burglary (8 percent) also increased but at nowhere near the levels for other property offenses. Women's involvement in violent offenses did not deviate from the earlier pattern. In 1975, women accounted for 10.3 percent of Type I violent offense arrests; in 1987, women accounted for 11.1 percent of those arrests.

Thus, the overall pattern of women's participation in criminal activities has not changed dramatically since 1975. The increase observed in the 1980s was for the same types of offenses reported earlier: property and white-collar crimes that women now have greater opportunities and skills to commit. There is no evidence that women have been any more involved in organized crime than they were at earlier times or that they have become more violent and aggressive than they were in the past.

Has there been a difference in the manner in which the courts have responded to female offenders? In 1975, Simon reported the reactions of criminal court judges interviewed in the Midwest and commented, "Most of the judges treat women more leniently than they do men. They are more inclined to recommend probation rather than imprisonment, and if they sentence a woman, it is usually for a shorter time than if the crime had been committed by a man" (Simon 1975, 109). The profile reported in this edition shows that judges are still inclined to treat women more gently than they do men. They believe today, as they did in 1975, that incarceration for a woman is far more degrading than for a man. They also believe that women are less likely than men to be repeat offenders.

The federal judicial statistics and those available from the states of California, Pennsylvania, and New York reveal a pattern that is consistent with recent arrest data—namely, that there has been an increase in the percentage of women charged with and convicted of property offenses. For example, the percentage of women convicted in federal courts increased by 6.4 percent, from 10.8 percent in 1979 to 17.2 percent in 1987. In 1987, 20 percent of the fraud, 49 percent of the embezzlement, 24 percent of the larceny, and 29 percent of the forgery convictions were of women. In the state courts, women accounted for 23 percent of the larceny convictions in California, 26 percent in New York, and 24 percent in Pennsylvania. In each of those states, women were convicted of less than 10 percent of all Type I offenses in 1987.

Women still account for 5 percent of the prison population, and more women than men are housed in medium and minimum security prisons (84 percent versus 71 percent). But there have been changes in the conditions under which women do time. The vast discrepancies between women's and men's opportunities for vocational training and jobs for pay have diminished. Not only do all women prisons now offer academic classes, but they also offer a broader range of training in vocations that will help provide female inmates with jobs once they are released from prison. Some prisons also have industries that offer women an opportunity to earn money while doing time.

Perhaps even more dramatic than the improvement in the opportunities for vocational training and industry have been the accommodations available for women to spend time with their children. In some women's prisons, children may visit as often as at least once a week and stay for as long as eight hours per visit. Some have weekend programs. At least nineteen of the state and federal institutions responding to our survey also reported the availability of furlough programs whereby mothers may visit their children at home or in halfway houses. Since some 70 percent of female inmates are mothers of young children, these changes are probably most welcome.

In closing, we note again that women are more represented in official crime statistics today than they have been at any time since systemic national data have been available. Their criminal niche seems to be property offenses, especially white-collar offenses involving small to medium amounts of money. Such criminal activities appear to be most consistent with their skills and opportunities.

Appendix: A Comparative Perspective

I n the appendix to the first edition of *Women and Crime,* Simon compared female arrest rates in twenty-five countries (not including the United States) in 1963, 1968, and 1970 and noted that higher crime rates and higher arrest rates were apparent in the more economically developed and technologically advanced societies. She concluded:

> Having reached the era in which women are expected to be "into crime" as they are expected to be "into" many activities that were previously closed or deemed inappropriate or of no interest to them, the topic of female partici-pation in crime is one that should, and probably will, be explored in more depth in the next decade than it has been in the previous half century. Com-parative studies of the type only suggested by the comments in this appendix should provide interesting and useful insights into women's propensities, ca-pabilities, and behavior in criminal activities. (Simon 1975, 118)

The purposes of this appendix are to assess some of the propensities noted earlier, to explore whether the expected changes in women's participation in crime have occurred, and to examine several theoretical frameworks relevant to understanding the pattern of female criminal involvement. Consistent with the thrust of the other chapters in the volume in which this appendix appeared as a chapter, it focuses on violent crime and examines the arrest rates of women for homicide and major larceny.[1] Our analysis also includes, for comparison pur-poses, minor larceny (for example, theft and receiving stolen goods) as a cate-gory of nonviolent property crime.

This appendix appeared as a chapter entitled "Gender and Violent Crime", co-authored with Sandra Bax-ter in *Violent Crime, Violent Criminals,* edited by Neil Alan Weiner and Marvin E. Wolfgang, Sage Pub-lications, Newbury Park, CA., 1989.

The following four questions are addressed here:

1. Have there been significant increases in female participation in criminal activities generally?

2. Have increases occurred in specific crime categories, and, if they have, are the crimes more likely to be of a violent nature or in the realm of property offenses?

3. If there have been increases, have they occurred across all societies?

4. Do any changes appear to be associated with women's changing educational and occupational status?

Review of the Literature

A major difficulty in integrating studies on women and violent crime stems from the absence of gender as a major analytic variable in contemporary theoretical approaches. As Harris (1977) notes, "This failure is more than merely methodological, precisely because it means that purportedly general theories of criminal deviance are now no more than special theories of male deviance" (p. 3). Criminological theories offer scant explanation for the long-observed disparity in the proportion of men and women who are arrested for violent and nonviolent crimes.[2] Consequently, these theories have not guided research on female criminal behavior, and the set of theoretically derived rival hypotheses is small.

The women's liberation movement of the mid-1960s generated a number of theoretical perspectives to fill the void. Building on Lombroso and Freud's arguments that female criminal behavior reflects role reversal, a number of scholars have proposed what Weis (1976) labels the *liberation theory* of female crime. Lombroso claimed that women who engage in crime are more masculine than their conformist sisters. Freudian theory holds that women who are not content with their roles as mothers and wives are maladjusted and that any manifestations of deviance, including their participation in criminal acts, reflect a "masculinity complex"—that is, penis envy. Adler (1975), as one of the liberation theory's chief proponents, wrote of this perspective:

The social revolution of the sixties has virilized its previously or presumably docile female segment. . . . The emancipation of women appears to be having a twofold influence on female juvenile crimes. Girls are involved in more drinking, stealing, gang activity, and fighting—behavior in keeping with their adoption of male roles. (pp. 87, 95)

A variant of this approach is the *human liberation* or *role convergence* theory of criminal behavior, which argues that criminal behavior is least frequent in settings in which boys are taught traditionally feminine values (for example, violence is never appropriate) and girls traditionally masculine values (for example, self-sufficiency) (see Wise 1967). This perspective was developed to account for the similarity and relative pettiness of deviant acts of middle-class boys and girls and the dissimilarity and violence apparent in the deviance of working-class boys and girls. Both of these approaches focus on the magnitude of differences in the socialization of women and men.

In contrast, the *opportunity*, or *role validation*, perspective proposes that women's criminal behavior is an illegitimate extension of the female role rather than a sign of masculinity (Weis 1976). For example, shoplifting and petty theft are extensions of the domestic consumption role of women; prostitution is an extension of the sexual role (Davis 1971). Hoffman-Bustamante (1973), Pollak (1950), and Simon (1975) have argued that opportunities for criminality are determined by sex roles. Women have committed primarily petty property crimes (for example, shoplifting) because these are the only opportunities available to housebound women whose major social role is that of a consumer. This perspective suggests that as women expand their roles, enter the labor force, and increase their education, they will experience the same opportunities and motivations to commit property crimes as do men. Advancements in the status of women per se should be associated with increases in their criminal conduct, which should, in turn, be reflected in an increase in the numbers of women arrested.

Hill and Harris (1981) labeled the opportunity explanation *objectivist* (that is, stemming from women's roles and status) and advocated a *subjectivist* explanation that stresses attitudes and interprets increases in women's criminality as reflecting changes in their self-perceptions. This dismissal of role (that is, social structural) approaches is in line with Harris's (1977) earlier contention that structural models cannot readily account for (1) the crime rate of women being much lower than that of men, or (2) the greater propensity of women to commit nonviolent property crimes rather than violent personal and property crimes. Durkheim's (1951) and Merton's (1968) *structural strain* theories predicted higher crime rates among women than among men because the former's traditional roles deny access to legitimate means of achievement, forcing them to become criminal innovators. Similarly, Harris (1977) contended, *differential opportunity* theory would interpret traditional sex roles as blocking access to both legitimate and illegitimate means. In their frustration, women would be expected to commit relatively more violent crimes than men. Neither of these expectations has been borne out in official U.S. police data or in the profile of offenders sketched by victimization surveys.

The women's liberation and opportunity theories continue to direct the bulk of research on women and crime today. Both perspectives argue that female crime rates should increase as women move toward greater equality with men in the social, economic, and political spheres. The opportunity approach, however, views changes that free women from solely home-based activities (such as getting a job and going to school) as simultaneously presenting opportunities for criminal, especially property, misconduct. The liberation perspective is more psychological and predicts increases in female crime as women's self-definitions change. Self-definitions are likely to change before actual changes in labor force and educational status occur.

The research design typically followed correlates changes in the status of women in the United States with *Uniform Crime Reports (UCR)* statistics over time. (The *UCR* has been published annually by the FBI since 1930 and presents data obtained from more than ten thousand law enforcement agencies across the country. These data include the number of arrests per year, the offenses for which suspects have been arrested, and the age, sex, and racial backgrounds of those arrested.) The problem with this design is that the study is couched in only one society, thus offering little variance in crime statistics and in the social, economic, or psychological factors thought to influence these statistics.

A richer design maximizes social structural variation by comparing national crime data derived from a large number of countries. Several researchers have followed this design (see, for example, Hartnagel 1982; Widom and Stewart 1986) but have drawn comparisons across a number of countries for only one year, which is a cross-sectional design. As discussed more fully in the next section, this strategy is problematic. A more rigorous approach, and the one used here, involves both comparative and longitudinal data. Crime rates are analyzed by country and across time, and conclusions are based on the empirical evidence from a widely varying set of countries over a long period of time.

Method

The data were drawn from the Correlates of Crime Archive (Bennett and Lynch 1986), which contains crime data printed in the International Police Organization's (Interpol's) biannual *International Crime Statistics*. Member countries voluntarily report the number of crimes recorded in total and by type (homicide, major larceny, minor larceny, fraud, and so on), the number of crimes cleared by arrest, and the number of offenders arrested (by gender and adult/juvenile status).

The validity and reliability of the Interpol data have been criticized by numerous researchers. Archer and Gartner (1984, 18) depicted Interpol data as "by far the least satisfactory." They were especially critical of the organization's arbitrary definitions of offense categories, which constitute a more serious threat to validity than the well-known tendency of member countries to use different operational definitions of types of crimes (Wellford 1974) or to underreport systematically (International Police Organization, cited in Bennett and Lynch 1986; Vigderhouse 1978). Archer and Gartner's (1984) contention was refuted by Bennett and Lynch's (1986) comparison of Interpol data (used in the Correlates of Crime Archive) with the figures Archer and Gartner collected directly from the nations. A test of the comparability between the two data sources found them virtually identical.

Whatever biases and inconsistencies exist in the Interpol figures, they are minimized when crime figures are analyzed for one nation over a considerable period of time. The data set analyzed here contains information on each of thirty-one countries from 1962 to 1980.

Six crime measures were defined using the Interpol data. The first three were total crimes (the total number of crimes reported to the police), overall arrests (the number of women and men arrested in all the crime categories reported to the police), and female arrests (the number of women arrested in all the crime categories). Each measure was converted to an annual rate through division by the nation's population for each year.[3] The three remaining crime measures separately calculated women's arrests for homicide, major larceny, and minor larceny. For each measure, the denominator was the number of women and men arrested for that offense category. The resulting figure was the percentage of women among those arrested for the offense. Increases in these measures were interpreted as greater proportions of women, and therefore lesser proportions of men, among arrested offenders.

There are known inconsistencies in what nations report as arrests. Some countries count only the people apprehended and others report only those formally arrested. The within-nation design of this study makes this cross-national variation acceptable if we assume that member nations do not change their definition of an arrested offender over time. We make this assumption.

Four social and demographic measures were examined. Female enrollment in secondary educational institutions was measured as the percentage of all secondary education students who were women in a given country. Female labor force participation was calculated as the percentage of women in the national labor force. Two other indexes measured social structural characteristics of the countries. The level of economic opportunity was measured by the per capita private consumption of the gross national product (GNP); the level of industrialization was indicated by the percentage of the labor force in industry. Other factors useful for testing the liberation and opportunity theories described here were not available over a period of years and for a large enough group of countries to be analytically useful.[4] These factors include the percentage of women employed in managerial and professional positions; the percentage of women who have completed the equivalent of four years of college or more; and statutes pertaining to women's rights to hold and inherit property, divorce, vote, or obtain an abortion.

Analysis and Findings

The first step in the analysis was to collapse the nineteen years' worth of data into three time frames: period A, 1962–1965; period B, 1969–1972; and period C, 1977–1980. This step was necessary to stabilize the rates by averaging out their minor year-to-date fluctuations.[5] The time periods were selected to represent the beginning, middle, and end of the nearly two decades for which data were available.

Crime Rates

Table A–1 presents the total crime rates for the thirty-one nations over the three time periods in descending order based on the crime rate in period A. The data show that the crime rates rose in twenty-three of the thirty-one nations and that there was a steeper increase in crimes reported between periods B and C than between periods A and B. Australia, the United States, Finland, and the Netherlands—all highly industrialized countries—showed the largest increases across the three periods. The eight countries in which crime rates fell (including Burma, Cyprus, Ivory Coast, and Kuwait) are developing nations.

Arrest Rates

Table A–2 shows the overall arrest rates in those same countries during the three time periods. Similar to the trend of the crime rates, the arrest rates increased in twenty of the thirty-one nations, but they increased more steeply between pe-

Table A–1
Total Crime Rates: 1962–1965, 1969–1972, 1977–1980

Country	Period A (1962–1965)	Period B (1969–1972)	Period C (1977–1980)	Group Means: Periods A, B, C	Rate Change: Periods A–B (%)	Rate Change: Periods B–C (%)
Sweden	4,885.58	7,853.51	10,235.68	7,658.26	+60.75	+30.33
New Zealand	4,696.58	6,291.36	9,634.57	6,874.17	+33.96	+53.14
Korea	3,580.52	1,404.41	1,486.84	2,157.26	−60.78	+5.87
Austria	3,297.63	3,634.55	4,285.04	3,739.07	+10.22	+17.90
West Germany	3,157.27	3,982.67	5,707.56	4,282.50	+26.14	+43.31
Israel	3,147.78	4,469.45	5,977.00	4,531.41	+41.99	+33.73
Denmark	3,059.91	5,704.32	6,958.66	5,240.96	+86.42	+21.99
Canada	3,052.67	5,375.08	7,149.32	5,189.02	+75.75	+33.26
Finland	2,899.60	6,137.32	10,132.46	6,389.79	+111.66	+65.10
Fiji	2,456.23	4,275.79	6,059.49	4,263.84	+74.08	+41.72
Libya	2,372.21	1,693.84	1,154.28	1,740.11	−28.60	−31.85
Japan	2,035.25	1,311.92	1,267.68	1,538.28	−35.54	−3.37
England/Wales	1,892.15	2,617.75	4,631.06	3,046.99	+38.35	+76.91
Australia	1,807.76	2,887.35	8,190.29	4,295.13	+59.72	+183.66
France	1,772.48	2,805.01	4,008.39	2,961.96	+58.25	+53.60
Kuwait	1,772.39	1,067.66	647.30	1,162.45	−39.76	−39.37
Luxembourg	1,619.12	1,990.07	2,649.29	2,086.16	+22.91	+33.13
Jamaica	1,592.44	1,756.17	2,461.58	1,936.73	+10.28	+40.17
Zambia	1,283.16	2,243.99	2,580.39	2,035.85	+74.88	+14.99
United States	1,269.96	3,058.11	5,309.87	3,212.65	+140.80	+73.63
Netherlands	1,269.35	2,390.63	4,339.49	2,666.49	+88.33	+81.52
Norway	1,241.43	1,919.28	2,636.73	1,932.48	+54.60	+37.38
Hong Kong	992.75	1,223.52	1,474.13	1,230.13	+23.25	+20.48
Cyprus	783.58	461.98	387.73	544.43	−41.04	−16.07
Burma	744.26	752.91	171.46	556.21	+1.16	−77.23
Philippines	690.05	66.07	121.92	292.68	−90.43	+84.53
Malawi	635.17	745.98	998.47	793.21	+17.45	+33.85
Ivory Coast	300.15	251.28	184.38	245.27	−16.28	−26.62
Malaysia	292.89	349.45	568.27	403.54	+19.31	+62.62
Sri Lanka	266.88	483.85	704.67	485.13	+81.30	+45.64
Nigeria	146.33	173.28	247.38	189.00	+18.42	+42.76
Median for time period	1,721.33	2,253.34	4,331.99	2,785.55	+30.91	+94.47
Mean for time period	1,903.66	2,560.28	3,634.24	2,699.39	+34.49	+41.95

Table A–2
Total Arrest Rates: 1962–1965, 1969–1972, 1977–1980

Country	Period A (1962–1965)	Period B (1969–1972)	Period C (1977–1980)	Group Means: Periods A, B, C	Rate Change: Periods A–B (%)	Rate Change: Periods B–C (%)
Israel	989.53	1,072.24	457.96	839.91	+8.36	−57.29
West Germany	769.39	944.93	1,287.40	1,000.57	+22.82	+36.24
New Zealand	719.54	1,063.83	1,740.67	1,174.68	+47.85	+63.62
Burma	585.79	459.38	313.72	452.96	−21.58	−31.71
Luxembourg	545.05	504.49	438.20	495.91	−7.44	−13.14
Austria	526.72	577.66	598.02	567.47	+9.67	+3.52
Finland	465.09	680.79	834.39	660.09	+46.38	+22.56
Kuwait	460.43	190.00	109.39	253.27	−58.73	−42.43
Korea	417.15	291.62	319.34	342.70	−30.09	+9.51
Australia	397.73	544.57	572.71	505.00	+36.92	+5.17
England/Wales	342.75	496.49	676.07	505.10	+44.85	+36.17
Netherlands	334.11	463.27	526.87	441.42	+38.66	+13.73
France	326.25	788.21	721.60	621.02	+141.60	−8.45
United States	325.39	539.43	896.40	587.07	+65.78	+66.18
Cyprus	290.58	188.33	125.19	201.37	−35.19	−33.53
Canada	278.56	379.17	791.55	483.09	+36.12	+108.76
Jamaica	276.03	725.11	918.12	639.75	+162.69	+26.62
Libya	269.77	224.38	176.89	223.68	−16.83	−21.16
Sweden	264.78	437.68	1,002.08	568.18	+65.30	+128.95
Zambia	263.68	208.38	206.49	226.18	−20.97	−0.91
Japan	259.45	189.13	198.10	215.56	−27.10	+4.74
Fiji	212.74	355.35	453.12	340.40	+67.03	+27.51
Norway	154.96	198.22	194.72	182.63	+27.92	−1.77
Hong Kong	147.10	185.47	239.84	190.80	+26.08	+29.31
Ivory Coast	130.02	161.96	115.91	135.96	+24.57	−28.43
Sri Lanka	121.08	239.20	153.11	171.13	+97.56	−35.99
Denmark	104.26	150.41	251.09	168.59	+44.26	+66.94
Philippines	102.82	55.09	43.83	67.25	−46.42	−20.44
Malawi	100.97	110.42	158.54	123.31	+9.36	+43.58
Malaysia	50.84	45.52	65.36	53.91	−10.46	+43.59
Nigeria	30.43	45.93	51.01	42.46	+50.94	+11.06
Median for time period	281.72	430.87	611.62	441.40	+52.94	+41.95
Mean for time period	331.06	403.76	472.18	402.34	+21.96	+16.95

riods A and B than between periods B and C. The nations showing the greatest increases continued to be in largely industrialized countries—Sweden, Canada, and the United States. Similarly, four of the nations with decreasing total crime rates—Kuwait, Cyprus, Burma, and the Philippines—showed the greatest declines in arrest rates.[6]

Female Arrest Rates

The total crime rate and the overall arrest rate figures provide some measure of the magnitude of offenses by men and women and the ability of police organizations to apprehend offenders. Within the national context provided by these data, it is interesting to examine the female arrest rates separately. The data in table A–3 show a steady increase in thirteen of the thirty-one countries. Only three nations—Kuwait, Israel, and Ivory Coast—showed consistent declines in female arrests. Across the thirty-one countries, women's arrests accounted for about one-eighth of the total arrests in each time period.

The repeated appearance of several countries (West Germany, Austria, and New Zealand) on the three lists of nations showing the greatest increases across the three periods in tables A–1 to A–3 led us to examine the extent to which female arrest rates rose or fell in accordance with total crime and overall arrest rates. Pearson's r values (a statistic that equates 1.0 at perfect correlation and zero at perfect independence) between total crime and female crime rates were similar to those reported for the overall arrest rates: $r = .63, .68,$ and $.73$ in periods A, B, and C, respectively. As could be expected, the correlations between overall arrest rates and female arrest rates were even higher: $r = .72, .88,$ and $.90$ in periods A, B, and C, respectively. The strength of the association among the three variables suggests that the factors influencing changes in a nation's crime and arrest rates also affect that nation's female arrest rates.

We turn next to an analysis of female arrests for homicide and major larceny. For purposes of comparison, we also report the percentage of female arrests for one nonviolent offense, minor larceny, which includes theft and receiving stolen goods.

Women's arrests for homicide, according to the data, decreased an average of 10 percent across the three time periods, and the decline was slightly steeper between periods A and B than between periods B and C (table A–4). Arrests for major larceny increased an average of 10 percent across the three time periods (table A–5). Nevertheless, women accounted for only about 10 out of every 100 homicide arrests and 4 out of every 100 major larceny arrests.

As hypothesized, an examination of the statistics in table A–6 reveals a

Table A-3
Total Female Arrest Rates: 1962–1965, 1969–1972, 1977–1980

Country	Period A (1962–1965)	Period B (1969–1972)	Period C (1977–1980)	Group Means: Periods A, B, C	Rate Change: Periods A–B (%)	Rate Change: Periods B–C (%)
West Germany	134.27	197.26	290.91	207.48	+46.91	+47.48
Austria	84.91	94.37	107.89	95.72	+11.14	+14.33
New Zealand	75.65	202.88	390.83	223.12	+168.18	+92.64
Luxembourg	66.92	77.35	69.65	71.31	+15.59	−9.95
Israel	63.32	53.32	51.84	56.16	−15.79	−2.78
England	52.42	72.90	151.37	92.23	+39.07	+107.64
Netherlands	48.63	67.01	67.92	61.19	+37.80	+1.36
Finland	48.02	77.81	97.34	74.39	+62.04	+25.10
United States	47.19	97.29	215.79	120.09	+106.17	+121.80
France	46.37	148.18	143.58	112.71	+219.56	−3.10
Australia	43.37	88.34	142.92	91.54	+103.69	+61.78
Japan	40.15	37.82	60.28	46.08	−5.80	+59.39
Sweden	36.11	62.01	138.11	78.74	+71.73	+122.72
Jamaica	34.38	157.06	62.49	84.64	+356.84	−60.21
Korea	32.32	26.69	31.67	30.23	−17.42	+18.66
Canada	26.70	60.16	115.60	67.49	+125.32	+92.15
Cyprus	19.02	8.94	9.11	12.36	−53.00	+1.90
Burma	15.92	17.57	26.14	19.88	+10.36	+48.78
Denmark	13.54	12.66	17.94	14.71	−6.50	+41.71
Norway	13.52	20.14	17.73	17.10	+48.22	−11.53
Libya	10.75	4.28	4.79	6.61	−60.19	+11.92
Fiji	7.21	12.80	19.28	13.10	+77.53	+50.63
Kuwait	7.16	7.09	4.85	6.37	−0.98	−31.59
Hong Kong	6.55	5.43	24.41	12.13	−17.10	+349.54
Zambia	4.46	3.20	5.01	4.22	−28.25	+56.56
Ivory Coast	4.28	4.12	3.78	4.06	−3.74	−8.25
Philippines	3.78	1.69	1.96	2.48	−55.29	+15.98
Sri Lanka	3.67	8.87	8.39	6.98	+141.69	−5.41
Malawi	2.17	2.73	4.80	3.23	+25.81	+75.82
Nigeria	1.11	3.08	2.67	2.29	+177.48	−13.31
Malaysia	0.77	0.69	0.79	0.75	−10.39	+14.49
Median for time period	34.27	28.18	46.09	36.18	−17.76	+63.52
Mean for time period	32.09	52.70	73.87	52.88	+64.24	+40.17

Table A–4

Percentage of Females Arrested for Homicide: 1962–1965, 1969–1972, 1977–1980

Country	Period A (1962–1965)	Period B (1969–1972)	Period C (1977–1980)	Group Means: Periods A, B, C	Rate Change: Periods A–B (%)	Rate Change: Periods B–C (%)
Norway	30.10	2.50	11.40	14.67	−91.66	+354.18
Denmark	25.00	14.00	12.40	17.13	−44.00	−11.43
England/Wales	23.40	15.80	13.70	17.63	−32.48	−13.29
Austria	23.20	18.80	20.70	20.90	−18.97	+10.11
New Zealand	22.90	14.00	10.30	15.73	−38.86	−26.43
Korea	21.70	17.50	17.30	18.83	−19.35	−1.14
West Germany	18.50	12.90	11.00	14.13	−30.27	−14.73
United States	18.20	15.60	13.70	15.81	−14.21	−12.07
Libya	18.00	15.90	9.70	14.53	−11.67	−38.99
Australia	16.60	12.80	14.00	14.47	−22.89	+9.38
Fiji	16.00	8.30	6.10	10.13	−48.13	−26.51
Jamaica	14.90	7.80	2.80	8.50	−47.65	−64.10
Japan	14.60	18.00	21.40	18.00	+23.29	+18.89
France	14.20	14.40	13.40	14.00	+1.41	−6.94
Finland	13.20	16.00	8.80	12.67	+21.21	−45.00
Netherlands	13.20	6.00	5.70	7.40	−42.86	−5.00
Canada	8.70	11.70	10.50	10.30	+34.48	−10.26
Malawi	7.50	4.80	11.90	8.07	−36.00	+147.92
Kuwait	7.00	6.40	11.50	8.30	−8.57	+79.69
Luxembourg	6.40	14.50	5.70	8.87	+126.56	−60.69
Ivory Coast	5.90	9.60	7.40	7.63	+62.71	−22.92
Israel	5.20	4.60	3.30	4.37	−11.54	−28.26
Nigeria	4.70	7.30	3.80	5.27	+55.32	−47.95
Sri Lanka	4.70	5.50	6.10	5.45	+17.87	+10.11
Sweden	4.10	12.10	9.70	8.63	+195.12	−19.83
Hong Kong	3.80	5.00	9.60	6.13	+31.58	+92.00
Malaysia	3.30	1.80	3.30	2.80	−45.45	+83.33
Zambia	2.80	1.00	0.30	1.37	−64.29	−70.00
Cyprus	2.10	23.30	12.50	12.63	+1,009.52	−46.35
Philippines	1.60	1.40	2.00	1.67	−12.50	+42.86
Burma	0.90	1.10	1.70	1.23	+27.59	+53.15
Mean	11.92	10.34	9.41	10.56	−13.31	−8.97

Table A-5

Percentage of Females Arrested for Major Larceny: 1962–1965, 1969–1972, 1977–1980

Country	Period A (1962–1965)	Period B (1969–1972)	Period C (1977–1980)	Group Means: Periods A, B, C	Rate Change: Periods A–B (%)	Rate Change: Periods B–C (%)
Denmark	16.00	7.90	5.10	9.66	−50.53	−34.19
Austria	10.30	8.50	5.30	8.03	−17.33	−37.34
Jamaica	9.10	23.90	4.70	12.55	+162.95	−80.21
France	9.00	8.70	7.30	8.32	−3.67	−15.38
Korea	6.80	2.40	1.40	3.51	−65.15	−43.04
Canada	4.80	6.10	5.70	5.49	+27.52	−6.92
Luxembourg	4.30	7.80	12.40	8.16	+79.03	+59.20
West Germany	4.00	3.60	5.40	4.30	−11.03	+51.27
Cyprus	3.90	2.20	4.50	3.53	−44.27	+104.11
United States	3.90	5.20	6.40	5.14	+33.42	+24.27
Netherlands	3.70	4.40	4.80	4.27	+18.48	+9.40
Finland	3.60	3.50	9.30	5.46	−3.31	+164.86
Israel	3.60	2.20	3.60	3.11	−39.83	+65.28
Norway	3.20	3.60	5.20	3.99	+13.25	+44.85
Australia	3.20	3.40	5.80	4.11	+7.62	+71.09
New Zealand	2.60	5.30	11.80	6.58	+101.52	+123.02
England/Wales	2.50	2.90	4.40	3.23	+15.85	+53.33
Sweden	2.10	2.70	4.60	3.14	+30.62	+68.50
Sri Lanka	2.00	3.40	6.40	3.93	+67.66	+90.50
Nigeria	2.00	2.10	2.10	2.07	+5.00	+0.95
Ivory Coast	1.80	3.00	1.90	2.26	+64.13	−36.42
Libya	1.60	2.30	2.80	2.24	+43.75	+22.61
Philippines	1.40	1.60	1.90	1.59	+15.44	+17.83
Hong Kong	1.20	0.80	0.60	0.87	−27.83	−25.30
Japan	1.10	1.70	6.80	3.21	+48.67	+305.95
Kuwait	1.10	1.80	2.20	1.68	+73.58	+16.85
Malawi	0.80	1.60	1.40	1.27	+92.68	−11.39
Burma	0.60	0.30	0.50	0.47	−50.79	+51.61
Fiji	0.60	0.80	0.90	0.75	+31.03	+21.05
Zambia	0.30	0.50	1.10	0.63	+35.29	+139.13
Malaysia	0.20	0.00	0.10	0.07	−100.00	0.00
Mean	3.58	3.99	4.39	3.99	+11.40	+10.09

Table A–6
Percentage of Females Arrested for Minor Larceny: 1962–1965, 1969–1972, 1977–1980

Country	Period A (1962–1965)	Period B (1969–1972)	Period C (1977–1980)	Group Means: Periods A, B, C	Rate Change: Periods A–B (%)	Rate Change: Periods B–C (%)
West Germany	21.60	31.20	29.70	27.50	+44.08	−4.59
Netherlands	20.90	25.20	22.00	22.68	+20.65	−12.63
Austria	20.80	25.90	25.30	23.98	+24.40	−2.05
Sweden	20.40	19.80	21.60	20.58	−3.04	+9.31
United States	20.30	22.40	30.60	24.43	+10.66	+36.49
England/Wales	19.40	19.10	28.40	22.31	−1.39	+48.46
Japan	18.80	22.30	34.30	25.11	+18.60	+54.25
Luxembourg	18.20	24.60	17.60	20.14	+35.00	−28.61
Jamaica	14.90	18.60	11.50	14.98	+25.13	−38.51
France	14.90	17.70	18.10	16.89	+19.39	+2.09
Finland	14.40	16.30	11.50	14.07	+13.12	−29.45
Norway	13.60	18.50	14.30	15.47	+35.36	−22.38
Australia	12.10	19.20	31.90	21.07	+58.20	+66.23
New Zealand	11.70	25.80	25.30	20.96	+120.10	−2.09
Cyprus	10.20	6.00	10.00	8.72	−41.64	+67.00
Canada	9.70	16.50	15.00	13.70	+69.69	−9.17
Korea	9.50	9.20	8.10	8.95	−2.94	−12.34
Israel	8.10	7.10	13.20	9.46	−12.00	+85.65
Burma	6.00	6.90	14.10	8.98	+15.03	+104.21
Philippines	5.30	5.10	7.60	6.03	−3.75	+48.54
Denmark	4.90	4.70	5.90	5.16	−3.49	+25.96
Hong Kong	4.50	4.10	18.20	8.93	−10.13	+345.34
Fiji	4.30	4.50	5.90	4.90	+5.59	+29.58
Nigeria	4.10	7.60	6.10	5.93	+84.88	−19.26
Sri Lanka	3.90	3.60	4.30	3.92	−6.49	+19.44
Ivory Coast	3.20	1.90	3.00	2.68	−41.25	+56.91
Libya	3.10	1.60	2.80	2.51	−47.57	+74.07
Malawi	2.60	2.80	3.40	2.90	−5.77	+21.82
Zambia	1.90	2.70	4.50	3.04	+38.14	+67.91
Kuwait	1.80	4.70	5.00	3.80	+161.80	+6.22
Malaysia	1.70	1.60	1.50	1.59	−8.19	−4.46
Mean	10.90	13.10	14.80	13.00	+31.70	+31.50

higher percentage of females arrested for minor larceny than for homicide (except in period A) and major larceny and a steady increase across the three time periods. On the whole, women accounted for about 13 out of every 100 arrests for minor larceny.

Even for minor larceny, the most frequent of the three offense types, the female arrest rate was only one-eighth that of the male arrest rate. The expectations of the liberation theorists—that by the 1980s, women would be involved in property offenses at a level comparable to that of men—were far from realized. Even in nations with the highest female minor larceny arrest rates—the United States, West Germany, and Japan—women accounted for less than one-third of such arrests.[7]

The data presented thus far show that crime rates and arrest rates increased at about the same pace and that the female arrest rates correlated strongly with the overall arrest rates. Examination of the data on female involvement in the major violent offense category showed a slight decline in the overall percentage of female homicide arrests across the three time periods. Female arrests for major larceny remained steady at a relatively low percentage. Female arrests for minor larceny increased more steeply than for major larceny but did not attain the levels anticipated by many researchers in the 1970s.

Societal Correlates of Crime

The opportunity, liberation, and social structural perspectives provide theories about the relationship between the percentage of women arrested for violent and property offenses and the socioeconomic and demographic characteristics of their societies. The demographic variables of interest are the percentages of women in the labor force and in institutions of higher education. These are direct indicators of women's freedom from their traditional domestic role. The socioeconomic variables are levels of industrialization and economic opportunity that measure the society-wide possibilities for women and men alike.

Durkheim's (1951) and Merton's (1968) structural strain theory predicted higher violent female crime rates in those societies in which there is greater suppression of women's rights. As women feel more downtrodden and blocked in their aspirations for social and economic equality with men, they are more likely to innovate by committing violent acts against those whom they view as the sources of their oppression. Thus, women in societies that do not allow divorce, that forbid them to inherit or hold property, that bar them from participation in institutions of higher education or in various labor markets, and that are not highly industrialized and offer few economic opportunities to their citizens are expected to be more likely to commit homicide and major larceny than are women in societies in which they enjoy the full rights of citizenship.

Conversely, high rates of female property offenders are likely to characterize societies that support female participation in higher education and the labor force, provide economic opportunities generally and as the result of industrialization, and give women political rights (for example, the right to vote), social rights (for example, divorce), and economic rights (for example, inheritance and the right to hold property in one's own name).

This phase of the analysis was directed at testing two theories: (1) women's propensities to commit violent offenses are negatively correlated with their labor force participation, enrollment in secondary education institutions, the nation's level of industrialization, and the nation's level of economic opportunity; and (2) women's propensities to commit property crimes are positively related to these same indicators.

Examining first, in table A–7, the correlations between female labor force participation and the percentage of females arrested for the three offenses, we found no strong correlations (.5 or above) in any of the three time periods. The strongest relationship was between minor larceny and female labor force participation ($r = .43$) in period C. The table also shows a strong relationship between

Table A–7

Pearson Product Moment Correlations between Crime and Societal Variables: 1962–1965, 1969–1972, 1977–1980

	Period A (1962–1965)	Period B (1969–1972)	Period C (1977–1980)
Correlation between female labor participation and the following:			
Female homicide arrests	0.07	0.12	0.10
Female major larceny arrests	0.23	0.12	0.18
Female minor larceny arrests	0.28	0.26	0.43
Correlation between female enrollment in secondary education and the following:			
Female homicide arrests	0.20	0.14	0.56
Female major larceny arrests	0.22	0.01	0.19
Female minor larceny arrests	0.51	0.45	0.36
Correlations between level of industrialization and the following:			
Female homicide arrests	0.37	0.40	0.51
Female major larceny arrests	0.50	0.40	0.46
Female minor larceny arrests	0.68	0.66	0.70
Correlations between level of economic opportunity and the following:			
Female homicide arrests	0.31	0.35	0.54
Female major larceny arrests	0.57	0.42	0.65
Female minor larceny arrests	0.56	0.53	0.65

females attending institutions of secondary education and female homicide arrests ($r = .56$) in period C. Overall, the top half of table A–7 shows little support for either theory.

In addition to the two demographic indicators, we also arrayed societies by levels of economic opportunity (the private consumption of the gross domestic product divided by the population) and industrialization (the percentage of the work force engaged in industry). Societies that are industrialized and measure high in economic opportunity offer women more important roles outside the home, which may in turn provide opportunities for criminal activities. Computing correlations between each of those measures and female homicide, major larceny, and minor larceny, we found many more strong relationships than for the demographic variables. Consistently high positive correlations were found between female minor larceny and both societal indicators in all three time periods. The data provide strong support for the second theory. The first theory—that job and labor force opportunities are negatively related to violent crimes by women—is clearly not supported. Not only are the correlation coefficients not negative, as would be expected, but they are occasionally strongly positive.

Conclusion

The data show that, over the nineteen-year time span, there were comparable levels of increase among crime, arrest, and female arrest rates from 1962 through 1980. The fears raised in the late 1960s and early 1970s that women's participation in crime would soon be commensurate with their representation in the population clearly were not realized. For homicide and major larceny, the percentages of female offenders actually decreased slightly. Thus, at least among the thirty-one countries for which longitudinal data were available, women continued to play relatively minor roles in those societies' violent criminal activities.

We found little support for the social structural theory of Durkheim (1951) and Merton (1968) that women would commit more violent crimes in less socially and economically progressive nations. We also discovered that the nonviolent crime of minor larceny does not correlate with changes in women's educational and work status, as the liberation and opportunity perspectives theorized, as strongly as it does with more general measures of societal economic opportunity. Interestingly, female arrests for the violent offenses of homicide and major larceny also were positively related to societal opportunity.[8]

The data presented here are an improvement over what has appeared in much of the comparative literature on women's participation in criminal activities in that we have marshaled longitudinal crime statistics over a nineteen-year time span for thirty-one countries. In addition to the crime and arrest statistics for violent offenses and one property offense, we presented data on four social and demographic characteristics: the percentage of females in the labor force, the percentage of female attending institutions of secondary education, the level of economic opportunity as measured by the per capita private consumptions of the GNP, and the level of industrialization as measured by the percentage of the labor force in industry. We used these measures because they permit hypothesis testing about female crime rates under different conditions and because they were available over the nineteen-year time span and for the thirty-one countries for which we had crime data.

We recognize that these are not the best measures. To make a more definitive test of the relationship between women's status and their crime patterns and rates in different societies over time, we need better statistics (for example, the number of women in each country's population, so that the female arrest rates can be calculated on the basis of the total female population) and more sensitive socioeconomic and sociopolitical indicators (such as women's rights to hold and inherit property, testify in court, divorce, abort unwanted babies, vote, and hold public office, as well as the percentage of women in the labor force in professional and managerial positions, the percentage of women who have completed at least four years of postsecondary education, and marriage and birth rates).

All of these measures together over two or three decades and for a wide range of countries would provide more definitive answers to questions we and many other researchers ask about the relationship between the status of women in a society; the roles they play; the political, social, and economic rights they enjoy; and the types and levels of crime they commit. With a sufficiently long time period, the changes in women's status and roles could be related to changes, or the lack thereof, in their participation in crime. These data are being collected in a more systematic manner, and we hope that future researchers will use them.

Notes

1. Major larceny is considered a violent offense because it includes robbery with dangerous aggravating circumstances.
2. In addition to homicide, major larceny, and minor larceny, the other offense categories are fraud, counterfeiting, drug offenses, and a miscellaneous category of offenses not including the six cited here.
3. Unfortunately, data on the number of women in each nation's population were not routinely available, so the female arrest rates were calculated using total population as the denominator.
4. World Bank and United Nations publications were the sources for the annual data on the number of women enrolled in secondary educational institutions, the level of economic oppor-

tunity, and the level of industrialization in a nation. The International Labor Organization published the data on female labor force participation.

5. Grouping the data in this fashion reduced the autocorrelation effect present in the time-series data and enabled unbiased correlation coefficients to be calculated between two data trends grouped in identical time period categories.

6. Pearson product moment correlation coefficients were calculated between the crime rates and the overall arrest rates for the three time periods. The coefficients were quite strong: $r = .73$, .73, and .75 for periods A, B, and C, respectively.

7. In computing Spearman's rank order correlations between the percentages of female arrests for homicide, major larceny, and minor larceny within each time period, we found the following:

	A	B	C
Homicide and major larceny	.44	.45	.39
Homicide and minor larceny	.38	.47	.47
Major and minor larceny	.65	.59	.59

Overall, the strongest relationship in each time period was between major and minor larceny. The former category, as we have noted, involves both violent and property offenses.

8. This study did not explore lagging variables during the analysis. The correlations were calculated within the same year, such that women's larceny in Sweden in 1976 was correlated with the arrest, demographic, and socioeconomic variables as measured for 1976. It may be that criminal behavior is a response to a preexisting condition and the crime data for 1976 should be correlated with the other variables as measured for 1975 or even earlier.

References

Abbott, Sidney, and Barbara Love. 1971. "Is Women's Liberation a Lesbian Plot?" In V. Gornick and B. Moran, etc. *Women in Sexist Society*, 601–621. New York: Basic Books.

Adler, Freda. 1975. *Sisters in Crime: The Rise of the New Female Criminal*. New York: McGraw-Hill.

American Correctional Association. 1988. 1989 Directory of Juvenile and Adult Correctional Departments, Institutions, Agencies and Paroling Authorities. Laurel, Md.

Anthony, Debra. 1973. "Judges Perceptions of Women Offenders and Their Own Actions Toward Women Offenders." Unpublished master's thesis. Urbana-Champaign: University of Illinois.

Archer, Dane, and Rosemary Gartner. 1984. *Violence and Crime in Cross-National Perspective*. New Haven, Conn.: Yale University Press.

Arditi, R.R.F. Goldberg, Jr., M.M. Hartle, J.H. Peters, and W.R. Phelps. 1973. "The Sexual Segregation of American Prisons: Notes." *Yale Law Journal* 82, 1229–1273.

Bartel, Ann P. 1979. "Women and Crime: An Economic Analysis" *Economic Inquiry* 17 (January): 29–51.

Baunach, Phyllis Jo. 1979. "Mothering from Behind Prison Walls." Paper presented to the American Society of Criminology.

Bennett, Richard, and James P. Lynch. 1986. *Does A Difference Make a Difference: Comparing Cross-National Crime Indicators*. Washington, D.C.: American University.

Bianchi, Suzanne M., and Daphne Spain. 1986. *American Women in Transition*. New York: Russell Sage Foundation.

Black, Donald. 1976. *The Behavior of Law*. New York: Academic Press.

Box, Steven. 1983. *Power, Crime, and Mystification*. London: Tavistock.

Box, Steven, and Chris Hale. 1983. "Liberation/Emancipation, Economic Marginalization, or Less Chivalry: The Relevance of Three Theoretical Arguments to Female Crime Patterns in England and Wales, 1951–1980." *Criminology* 22, no. 4: 473–497.

Burkhart, K. 1973. *Women in Prison*. New York: Doubleday.

Cernkovich, Stephen A., and Peggy Giordano. 1979. "Delinquency, Opportunity and Gender" *Journal of Criminal Law and Criminology* 70(Summer): 145–151.

Chafe, W.H. 1972. *The American Woman*. New York: Oxford University Press.

Chapman, Jane R. 1980. *Economic Realities and the Female Offender*. Lexington, Mass.: Lexington Books.

Chesney-Lind, Meda. 1986. "Women and Crime: The Female Offender." *Signs: Journal of Women in Culture and Society* 12, no. 1: 78–96.

Chesney-Lind, Meda. 1987. "Female Offenders: Paternalism Reexamined." In Laura L. Crites and Winifred L. Hepperle, eds. *Women, The Courts, and Equality,* 114–139. Newbury Park, Calif.: Sage Publications.

Cressey, Donald R. 1953. *Other People's Money: A Study in the Social Psychology of Embezzlement.* Reprinted in 1973. Montclair, N.J.: Patterson Smith.

Crites, Laura L., and Winifred L. Hepperle, eds. 1987. *Women, the Courts and Equality.* Newbury Park, Calif: Sage Publications.

Daly, Kathleen. 1983. *Order in the Court: Gender and Justice.* Washington, D.C.: National Institute of Justice.

Daly, Kathleen. 1987. "Discrimination in Criminal Courts: Family, Gender, and the Problem of Equal Treatment." *Social Forces* 66: 152–175.

Daly, Kathleen. 1989a. "Neither Conflict nor Labeling nor Paternalism Will Suffice: Intersections of Race, Ethnicity, Gender and Family in Criminal Court Decisions" *Crime and Delinquency* 35, no. 1: 136–168.

Daly, Kathleen. 1989b. "Rethinking Judicial Paternalism: Gender, Work-Family Relations, and Sentencing" *Gender and Society* 3, no. 1: 9–36.

Daly, Kathleen. 1989c. "Gender and Varieties of White-Collar Crime." *Criminology* 27, no. 4: 769–793.

Daly, Kathleen, and Meda Chesney-Lind. 1988. "Feminism and Criminology" *Justice Quarterly* 5, no. 4: 101–143.

Datesman, Susan, and Frank R. Scarpetti. 1980. *Women, Crime and Justice.* New York: Oxford University Press.

Davis, K. 1971. "Prostitution." in R.K. Merton and R. Nisbet. eds. *Contemporary Social Problems.* New York: Harcourt Brace.

DeFleur, Lois B. 1975. "Biasing Influences on Drug Arrest Records: Implications for Deviance Research." *American Sociological Review* 40, no. 1: 88–103.

Deming, Richard. 1977. *The New Criminals.* New York: Dell.

Durkheim, Emile. 1951. *Suicide: A Study in Sociology.* John A Spaulding and George Simpson, trans. New York: Free Press. (original work published 1897).

Epstein, C., and W. Goode, eds. 1973. *The Other Half.* Englewood Cliffs, N.J.: Prentice Hall.

Farley, Reynolds and Walter R. Allen. 1987. *The Color Line and the Quality of Life in America.* New York: Russell Sage Foundation.

Farrington, D.P., and A.M. Morris. 1983. "Sex, Sentencing and Reconviction." *British Journal of Criminology* 23, no. 3: 229–248.

Feinman, Clarice. 1976. "Inmate Demographic Profile, March 1975–December 1975." In *Women's Development Unit Project Annual Report, January 1, 1975–April 6, 1979,* 18. New York: New York City Correctional Institution for Women.

Feinman, Clarice. 1986. *Women in the Criminal Justice System.* 2nd ed. New York: Praeger.

Fenster, C. 1977. "Differential Dispositions: A Preliminary Study of Male-Female Partners in Crime." Paper presented to the Annual Meeting of the American Society of Criminology, Atlanta, Ga.

Freeman, Jo. 1973. "The Origins of the Women's Liberation Movement." *American Journal of Sociology* 78, no. 4: 798–812.

Freeman, Jo. 1985. "The Women's Liberation Movement: Its Origins, Structures, Impact, and Ideas," In Jo Freeman, ed. *Women: A Feminist Perspective.* Palo Alto, Calif.: Mayfield Publishing Co.

Ghali, M., and M. Chesney-Lind. 1986. "Gender Bias and the Criminal System" *Sociology and Social Research* 70, no. 2: 164–171.

Giallombardo, R. 1966. *Society of Women: A Study of a Women's Prison*. New York: John Wiley and Sons.

Glick, Ruth M., and Virginia V. Neto. 1977. *National Study of Women's Correctional Programs*. Washington, D.C.: U.S. Government Printing Office.

Gora, Joanne G. 1982. *The New Female Criminal: Empirical Reality or Social Myth?* New York: Praeger.

Gornick, Vivian, and Barbara Moran, eds. 1971. *Woman in Sexist Society*. New York: Basic Books.

Grasmick, Harold G., Nancy J. Finley, and Deborah L. Glaser. 1984. "Labor Force Participation, Sex-Role Attitudes and Female Crime." *Social Science Quarterly* 65, no. 3: 703–718.

Hagan, John. 1985. "Toward a Structural Theory of Crime, Race and Gender: The Canadian Case." *Crime and Delinquency* 31, no. 1: 129–146.

Hagan, John., A.R. Gillis, and J. Simpson. 1985. "The Class Structure of Gender and Delinquency: Toward a Power-Control Theory of Common Delinquent Behavior." *American Journal of Sociology* 90, no. 6: 1151–1178.

Hagan, John, J.H. Simpson, and A.R. Gillis. 1979. "The Sexual Stratification of Social Control: A Gender-Based Perspective on Crime and Delinquency." *British Journal of Sociology* 30, no. 1: 25–38.

Harris, A.R. 1977. "Sex and Theories of Deviance: Toward a Functional Theory of Deviant Type-Scripts." *American Sociological Review* 42: 3–16.

Hartnagel, T.F. 1982. "Modernization, Female Social Roles, and Female Crime: A Cross-National Investigation." *Sociological Quarterly* 23: 477–490.

Heidensohn, Frances M. 1985. *Women and Crime: The Life of the Female Offender*. London: Macmillan Pub. Ltd.

Hill, G.D., and A.R. Harris. 1981. "Changes in the Gender Patterning of Crime, 1953–1977: Opportunity vs. Identity." *Social Science Quarterly* 62: 658–671.

Hoffman-Bustamante, Dale. 1973. "The Nature of Female Criminality." *Issues in Criminology* 8 (Fall): 117–136.

Kempinen, Cynthia. 1979. "Changes in the Sentencing Patterns of Male and Female Criminal Defendants." *The Prison Journal* 63, no. 2: 3–11.

Klein, D., and J. Kress. 1976. "Any Woman's Blues: A Critical Overview of Women, Crime, and Criminal Justice." *Crime and Social Justice* 5: 34.

Koontz, B. 1971. "Public Hearings on Women and Girl Offenders." *D.C. Commission on the Status of Women*, November 4, 1971.

Kornhauser, Anne. 1989. "Male-Only 'Club Feds' Hit in Suit." *Legal Times* 12, no. 29:1, 25.

Krohn, Marvin D., James P. Curry, and Shirley Nelson-Kilger. 1983. "Is Chivalry Dead? An Analysis of Changes in Police Dispositions of Males and Females." *Criminology* 21, no. 3: 417–437.

Kruttschnitt, Candace. 1982. "Women, Crime, and Dependency: An Application of the Theory of Law." *Criminology* 19, no. 4: 495–513.

Kruttschnitt, Candace. 1984 "Sex and Criminal Court Dispositions: The Unresolved Controversy." *Research in Crime and Delinquency* 21, no. 3: 213–232.

Kruttschnitt, Candace. 1980–1981. "Social Status and Sentences of Female Offenders." *Law and Society Review* 15, no. 2: 247–265.

Leonard, Eileen. 1982. *Women, Crime and Society: A Critique of Theoretical Criminology*. New York: Longman, Inc.

Leventhal, Gloria. 1977. "Female Criminology: Is Women's 'Lib' to Blame?" *Psychological Reports* 41: 179–182.

Lewis, Diane K. 1981. "Black Women Offenders and Criminal Justice: Some Theoretical Considerations." In Marguerite Warren, ed. *Comparing Female and Male Offenders*. Beverly Hills, Calif.: Sage Publications.

Lewis, Diane K., and Laura Bresler. 1981. *Is There A Way Out? A Community Study of Women in the San Francisco County Jail*. San Francisco: Unitarian Universalist Service Committee.

Mann, Coramae Richey. 1984. *Female Crime and Delinquency*. Tuscaloosa: University of Alabama Press.

McGowan, Brenda, and Karen Blumenthal. 1978. *Why Punish the Children? A Study of Women Prisoners*. Hackensack, N.J.: National Commission on Crime and Delinquency.

Merton, Robert K. 1968. *Social Theory and Social Structure*. Glencoe, Ill.: Free Press.

Messerschmidt, James W. 1986. *Capitalism, Patriarchy and Crime: Toward a Socialist Feminist Criminology*. Totowa, N.J.: Rowman and Littlefield.

Miller, Eleanor M. 1985. *Street Woman*. Philadelphia: Temple University Press.

Millett, K. 1968. *Sexual Politics*. Garden City, N.Y.: W.W. Norton & Co.

Millett, K. 1973. *Prostitution Papers*. New York: Avon.

Musolino, Angela. 1988. "Judge's Attitudes Toward Female Offenders." Unpublished manuscript.

Naffine, Ngaire. 1987. *Female Crime: The Construction of Women in Criminology*. Boston: Allen and Unwin.

Nagel, Ilene H., John Cardascia, and Catherine Ross. 1982. "Sex Differences in the Processing of Criminal Defendants." In D. Kelly Weisberg, ed. *Women and the Law*. Cambridge, Mass.: Schenkman Publishing Co.

Nagel, S.S., and L.J. Weitzman. 1971. "Women as Litigants." *Hastings Law Journal* 23, no. 1: 171–198.

Norland, Stephen, and Neal Shover. 1978. "Gender Roles and Female Criminality." *Criminology* 15: 97–104.

Pollak, Otto. 1950. *The Criminality of Women*. Philadelphia: University of Pennsylvania Press.

Ryan, T.A. 1984. *Adult Female Offenders and Institutional Programs: A State of the Art Analysis*. Washington, D.C.: National Institute of Corrections.

Simon, Rita J. 1975. *Women and Crime*. Lexington, Mass.: Lexington Books.

Simon, Rita J., and Sandra Baxter. 1989. "Gender and Violent Crime." In Neil Weiner and Marvin Wolfgang, eds. *Violent Crime, Violent Criminals*. Beverly Hills, Calif.: Sage Publications.

Simon, Rita J., and Jean M. Landis. 1989. "Poll Report: Attitudes About a Woman's Place and Role." *Public Opinion Quarterly* 53, no. 2: 265–276.

Simon, Rita J., and Navin Sharma. 1979. *The Female Defendant in Washington, D.C.: 1974 and 1975*. Washington, D.C.: Institute for Law and Social Research.

Simpson, S.S. 1989. "Feminist Theory, Crime and Justice." *Criminology* 27, no. 4: 605–632.

Singer, L. 1973. "Women and the Correctional Process." *American Criminal Law Review* 11 (Winter): 295.

Smart, Carol. 1979. "The New Female Criminality: Reality or Myth?" *British Journal of Criminology* 19, no. 1: 50–59.

Smart, Carol. 1976. *Women, Crime and Criminology: A Feminist Critique*. Boston: Routledge and Kegan Paul.

Spohn, Cassia, John Gruhl, and Susan Welch. 1987. "The Impact of the Ethnicity and Gender of Defendants on the Decision to Reject or Dismiss Felony Charges." *Criminology* 25, no. 1: 175–191.

Spohn, Cassia, Susan Welch, and John Gruhl. 1985. "Women Defendants in Court: The Interaction Between Sex and Race in Convicting and Sentencing." *Social Science Quarterly* 66, no. 1: 178–185.

Stallard, K., B. Ehrenreich, and H. Sklar. 1983. *Poverty and the American Dream*. Boston: South End Press.

Stanford, Rosemary, Manuel Vega, and Ira J. Silverman. 1982. "A Study of the Female Forger." *Journal of Offender Counseling, Services and Rehabilitation* 6, no. 4: 71–81.

Steffensmeier, Darrell J. 1978. "Crime and the Contemporary Woman: An Analysis of Changing Levels of Female Property Crime, 1960–1975." *Social Forces* 57, no. 2: 566–584.

Steffensmeier, Darrell J. 1980a. "Assessing the Impact of the Women's Movement on Sex-Based Differences in the Handling of Adult Criminal Defendants." *Crime and Delinquency* 26, no. 3: 344–357.

Steffensmeier, Darrell J. 1980b. "Sex Differences in Patterns of Adult Crime, 1965–1977: A Review and Assessment." *Social Forces* 58, no. 3: 1080–1108.

Steffensmeier, Darrell J. 1982. "Trends in Female Crime: It's Still a Man's World." In B.R. Price, and N.J. Sokoloff, eds. *The Criminal Justice System and Women*. N.Y.: Clark Boardman Co., Ltd.

Steffensmeier, Darrell J., and Emilie A. Allan. 1988. "Sex Disparities in Arrests by Residence, Race, and Age: An Assessment of the Gender Convergence/Crime Hypothesis." *Justice Quarterly* 5, no. 1: 53–80.

Steffensmeier, Darrell, and John H. Kramer. 1982. "Sex-Based Differences in the Sentencing of Adult Criminal Defendants." *Sociology and Social Research* 66, no. 3: 289–304.

Steffensmeier, Darrell, and Robert M. Terry. 1986. "Institutional Sexism in the Underworld: A View from the Inside." *Sociological Inquiry* 56, no. 3: 304–322.

Stimpson, C., 1971. "'Thy Neighbor's Wife, Thy Neighbor's Servants': Women's Liberation and Black Civil Rights." In Vivian Gornick and Barbara K. Moran, eds. *Woman in Sexist Society*, 622–657. New York: Basic Books.

Temen, Linda. 1973. "Discriminatory Sentencing of Women Offenders." *Criminal Law Review* 11.

Thorton, Wm. E., and Jennifer James. 1979. "Masculinity and Delinquency Revisited." *British Journal of Criminology* 19: 225–241.

Uniform Crime Reports: Crime in the United States, 1987. Washington, D.C.: U.S. Department of Justice, Federal Bureau of Investigation.

U.S. Comptroller General. 1980. *Women In Prison: Inequitable Treatment Requires Action*. Washington, D.C.: General Accounting Office.

Vigderhouse, G. 1978. "Methodological Problems Confronting Cross-Cultural Criminological Research Using Official Data." *Human Relations* 31: 229–247.

Visher, Christy. 1983. "Gender, Police Arrest Decisions, and Notions of Chivalry." *Criminology* 21, no. 1: 5–28.

Ward, D., M. Jackson, and E. Ward. 1968. "Crime and Violence By Women." *Crimes of Violence* 13, appendix 17. President's Commission on Law Enforcement and the Administration of Justice.

Ward, David, and Gene Kassebaum. 1965. *Women's Prisons*. Chicago: Aldine Publishing Co.

Weis, J.G. 1976. "Liberation and Crime: The Invention of the New Female Criminal." *Crime and Social Justice* 6 (Fall/Winter): 17–27.

Weisheit, Ralph, and Sue Mahan. 1988. *Women, Crime, and Criminal Justice*. Cincinnati, Oh.: Anderson Publishing Co.

Wellford, Charles R. 1974. "Crime and the Dimensions of Nations." *International Journal of Criminology and Penology* 2: 1–10.

Widom, Cathy S. 1979. "Female Offenders: Three Assumptions About Self-Esteem, Sex Role Identity and Feminism." *Criminal Justice and Behavior* 6: 365–382.

Widom, C.S., and A.J. Stewart. 1986. "Female Criminality and the Status of Women." *International Annals of Criminology* 24: 137–162.

Wise, N.B. 1967. "Juvenile Delinquency Among Middle-Class Girls." In E.W. Vaz, ed. *Middle-Class Juvenile Delinquency.* New York: Harper and Row.

Wooten, Lady Barbara. 1963. *Crime and Criminal Law.* New York: Macmillan.

Zietz, Dorthy. 1981. *Women Who Embezzle or Defraud: A Study of Convicted Felons.* New York: Praeger.

Index

About the Authors

Rita J. Simon is a University Professor at The American University. She has authored over a dozen books including *The Jury and the Defense of Insanity, The American Jury, Public Opinion and the Immigrant, Transracial Adoptees and Their Families* (with Howard Altstein), and *The Insanity Defense: A Critical Assessment of Law and Policy in the Post-Hinkley Era* (with David Aaronson). Professor Simon is a former editor of *The American Sociological Review* and of *Justice Quarterly*.

   Jean M. Landis is a doctoral candidate in the Sociology: Justice, Law and Society Program at The American University.